Possibilities II:

Stories From the Heart
That Feed The Mind

ISBN: 0-9641240-6-8

Published by

Brown Books, Inc.
16200 Dallas Parkway, Suite 225
Dallas, Texas 75248 U.S.A.

972-381-0009

www.brownbooks.com

FOREWORD

There are times in our lives that meaningful experiences occur, and like ripples in a pond, the effects resonate beyond the initial impact of the pebble.

In this edition of Oklahoma Speakers Association's (an official chapter of the National Speakers Association) anthology, *Possibilities II: Stories From the Heart That Feed The Mind*, you may find many "pebbles" that will touch your heart and give your mind the food necessary for lasting positive results!

You will see that these contributing professionals are experts in their chosen fields and each works with countless individuals across the globe each year to affect their still waters. Through powerful heartfelt messages they stimulate lasting positive effect as "pebbles" in the still waters of others' lives.

We hope that you find each chapter a resounding life-affecting "pebble" in one way or another and that you may feel moved to share this book with those around you . . . in your professional and personal life!

To learn more about or to get in contact with an author, please refer to the back of the book for individual contributing author information. Let them become lasting "pebbles" in your life . . . let them continue to feed both your heart and mind!

Best Wishes,
Jeffrey Magee, CSP/CMC
OSA 2001-2002 Co-President
Possibilities II, Editor
www.oklahomaspeakers.com

CONTENTS

The Neon Sign In The Sky

by Dr. Joani Bedore
Founder, PEACEMAKER Seminars Inc.

The Neon Sign In The Sky

by Dr. Joani Bedore
Founder, PEACEMAKER Seminars Inc.

The universe has a funny way of getting your attention.

First, it gently nudges you with quiet reminders. Then, it sends you odd coincidences and unexpected challenges. After that, it bombards you with close calls and near misses.

Finally, if you're still too thickheaded for even those signs, it demands your attention by lighting up the neon sign in the sky. At that point, you either pay attention or pay the price.

I failed to pay attention.

Passing out cold and falling flat on my face in front of an audience was not my idea of the way to launch a seminar company, but that's honestly what happened. To make matters worse, my sessions were being videotaped—in living color—on that muggy April morning when I pitched face-forward to the floor.

I never made it to the afternoon session, where the Peaceful Heart concepts were to be launched for the first time. I was in the emergency room instead.

How humiliating. How like the universe to actually drop the neon sign right on my head to slow me down and get me to ask for help. You'd think I'd have paid more attention to the warning signs earlier on . . . .

Back in January of 2001, I made the hard decision to give up my lifelong teaching career to start my own seminar company. I had some powerful ideas I wanted to share with others and decided it was time to get them out there.

At first, I just wanted to keep myself gainfully employed. It seemed simple enough—create the activities; select the music; market the seminar; do the trainings.

What could be easier?

But by the end of the first month, I was already in trouble. Unsettled by the insecurity of entrepreneurship, I was scared to get out there. An identical twin from a close-knit family of 13 people, I was truly uncomfortable with the idea of striking out on my own.

January came and went in a blinding flash. I barely remember sleeping. My days and nights were a jumbled whirl of business meetings, advice-gathering lunches, and self-study hours. I listened to about 70 audiotapes, watched over a dozen videos, and journaled my actions. Every single night, I poured over marketing, advertising, and sales books. I went to every networking meeting in town and eventually had more "to-do" lists than friends.

My sleep was fitful and interrupted. My meals were haphazardly thrown together and gulped hastily while I worked. I felt tired and seriously low on energy every single day in January, but didn't ask for help. I was determined to do this by myself if it killed me.

I ignored the gentle nudges and quiet reminders.

Surely it was just the fear and anticipation of starting something new. Though my universe was trying to get my attention and tell me to slow down and ask for help, I pressed on alone.

February was no better. As before, those quiet reminders continued to tug at me. My stomach hurt. My energy sagged. My body was weary. I decided to work around those signals, perceiving them as obstacles rather than warning signs. I redoubled my solitary efforts, working day and night to create PEACEMAKER Seminars Inc.

In early March, an exasperated friend reached over the table at lunch and shook me hard by my shoulders. She wanted to know what I had a burning desire to do.

Caught off guard, I replied that I wanted to work with others to help people create peaceful lives. She laughed, reminding me that I had chosen to work alone.

She was right—I had brushed off other people's offers to help me.

That got my attention.

The redesign of my dream started that afternoon. I decided to allow some friends to get certified to facilitate the brand-new Peaceful Heart Seminar.

That should have been the end of this story. You might have then concluded that I actually paid attention to the universe.

But that's not what happened.

Instead of divvying up the work between my many new partners, I kept right on handling it alone. I continued to get nowhere fast. It was a real grind.

I wanted to create an entirely different kind of seminar experience. We would take our time and explore a few powerful concepts in deeply relaxing ways with our participants. We would spoil our attendees with a magical day of self-renewal. We would teach simple stress and anger management skills to small groups of corporate leaders and workers. We would offer them compelling business reasons to become more peaceful at work and at home.

We would be a quiet alternative to the big seminar companies because we would stay in town and sit with our participants—working to create successful new ways to think and act. We would show them how to slow down and take care of themselves. We would help them create peaceful lives that worked on all levels. And we would give them practical concepts that they could use every day for the rest of their lives.

Ironically, I wanted to create exactly the type of peaceful heart experience that I most desperately needed in my life, though I hadn't realized it at the time.

Because of my refusal to respond to the first quiet nudges, my universe stepped up the pace of its messages. Odd coincidences and unexpected challenges cropped up frequently, but I didn't pay them much attention either.

The signals became more insistent.

The more tired I became, the more close calls and near

misses I had. Though my new facilitators volunteered to help, I brushed aside their offers. I could do it all myself.

It was now April, just a few weeks before I went down for the count. I had just tendered my resignation from my teaching position and was scared to death of the coming events.

The showcase was set for third week of April. I was furiously preparing and organizing the debut of our Peaceful Heart concepts, the ones I had left my lifelong teaching career to create. I wanted everything to go smoothly.

As the day drew near, I found I had more and more details to handle. I decided to put off shopping until after the showcase. That meant that I wouldn't be able to have my normally heavy breakfast on my presentation day. I'd settle for some watery instant oatmeal instead.

Bad decision.

That turned out to be the first of many bad decisions I made prior to, and on the morning of, my humiliating debut.

The night before the showcase, I was so excited about the event that my mind was busy going over every detail—which, of course, meant that I was getting less and less sleep. By the time morning dawned, I had been in bed for seven hours but asleep for only about three.

I started rushing around the second I awoke on that muggy April morning. Hastily, I showered and dressed, choosing a thick pale yellow sweater, a long-sleeved white turtleneck cut jaggedly at the midriff, and a pair of thick, navy blue dress slacks.

Another bad decision.

I had selected a lighter, cooler outfit the night before and had tried it on but inexplicably took it off at the last second and switched to the hotter one.

Absently, I ate my watery oatmeal. I don't remember gulping it down, but the bowl was in my soapy dishpan that night when I returned from the emergency room.

Feeling rushed and still hungry, I tossed a Gala apple into one of the bags. I knew I needed to eat a snack before lunch since I was burning so much energy. I planned to munch on it at the very first break and drink some water.

After my quick breakfast, I sped into high gear. My bags and boxes were already lined up by the front door, so I ran them quickly down to the car. With all the extra props I had, I made several trips. I was sweating profusely, but I thought I'd get some water later.

Then, as my ignition was turning over, a brilliant idea occurred to me. I decided to go back for my six-foot artificial tree.

Yet another bad decision.

Panting and grunting, I lugged it downstairs and jammed it into my little green Kia Rio. The leaves and a good number of odd branches hung out of the front passenger window as I slowly made my way across town. The air conditioner wasn't effective with the window rolled down so far. I was surprised at how hot it was.

Fifteen minutes later, and not a drop more hydrated, I arrived at the venue and started hauling all those heavy bags and boxes into the auditorium—alone. I waved off several offers to help from people setting up the registration table. They shrugged off my refusals and went back to their preparations.

I even lugged that tree in by myself, as awkward as that was.

Then I paced the stage repeatedly to get the microphone to stop squealing, all the while sweating and burning up more energy. Before my first session even began, I was dangerously overheated and in trouble.

Did I listen to the warning signs and ask for help?

No.

I needed to crash and burn to get the full impact of this lesson.

Though I had good sense to get myself some water, I can't say I actually drank it. It sat untouched on my table alongside my apple.

I continued setting up quickly and furiously—alone, of course.

As I was placing materials on the chairs, the doors opened and people flooded in. I had planned to sit down, cool down, and hydrate at that point, but seeing everyone arriving made me forget all that. My last moments were spent welcoming my participants.

The auditorium was unevenly ventilated. The stage area and the first three rows were about 10-15 degrees hotter than the rest of the room. Not seeing the event coordinator in the immediate vicinity, I decided to wait until the break to ask if she could get the thermostat adjusted. It didn't occur to me to ask someone else to do that for me.

The first session began without a hitch. The audio and videotaping clicked right into place, and the audience was settling in for a good morning with me. It was fun to be on stage after all those months of preparation. I was in my element, and I was happy.

And things were going well, too. The audience was laughing easily and often. I felt really happy about that. I introduced some of our local PEACEMAKER Seminars Inc. Visionary Facilitators, and they were well-received.

The talk progressed nicely, and except for the fact that I was seriously overheated and drained of energy and dangerously dehydrated, all was well.

I walked over to the water glass several times because I was boiling hot under those lights, but I never took a sip. Nor did I chomp down on my apple at the break, though a friend reminded me to. Someone got me talking on my way to the restroom and I simply forgot.

My second session started, but it did not progress quite as well. My stomach was growling angrily since I had neglected to feed it. It was definitely too late to run over and grab a few bites of my apple. I would just have to ignore the rumblings.

About twenty minutes passed. The front of the auditorium grew intensely hotter. I felt as though I were standing under a blast furnace. Sweating, I walked around more to cool myself off. It didn't work. I was burning up inside and out.

Suddenly, my left side started cramping. I couldn't figure out what was going on. I leaned against the railing to see if that would help. For a few moments, the pain subsided; then it returned with a vengeance.

When the first three rows of people fanned themselves furiously, I asked someone to cool us off. I remember getting a sip of water, but then it was back to the talk. We only had fifteen minutes left to cover a lot of ground.

Sweat was dripping off my brow, which was quite unusual. There was no way I could take off my sweater because my turtleneck had been raggedly cut off at the midriff. I would have to tough it out until lunch though my clothing was drenched.

By now, things seemed to be happening in slow motion. I began to feel seriously nauseated and very, very fatigued. I felt incredibly drowsy and slightly dizzy. Neither of those sensations was even remotely common for me. I looked around the stage for a chair. There was none. I hadn't noticed that before. Foggily, I plodded on with my talk, probably not making a whole lot of sense to the audience by that time.

My left side ached steadily. It felt as though someone were stabbing me with a knife. I tried to twist and bend so that the pain would stop. It was no use. The stabbing only intensified. That kept my mind off my thirst. I was too disoriented to realize that that one symptom of heat exhaustion was connected to the other.

I noticed that I was no longer perspiring. Since my sweater was wringing wet, this sudden dryness seemed like a welcomed relief.

With about nine minutes to go before the lunch break, the neon sign in the sky finally hit me over the head. I hadn't paid attention to the dozens of warning signs in the past four months (especially on this day), and it was time to pay the price.

In my last few seconds of consciousness on stage, I remember looking around for the absent chair once more; stupidly noticing my water and my apple on the front table; holding my side to see if I could stop the pain; repeating a garbled sentence; leaning against the railing to steady myself; dismissing a very surprised audience to go to lunch nine minutes early; seeing the darkness "tunnel in" rapidly between my eyes; and then blacking out. I fell face-forward onto the cement floor.

I regained consciousness in about three seconds as a small crowd of worried strangers and friends ran to the stage to help me.

The paramedics removed my sweater and shirt (so much for modesty), iced me down, made me drink fruit juice and eat my apple, bandaged my head, stabilized me, lifted me clumsily into a wheelchair, sent me up the chairlift, then turned me over to my best friend who quietly drove me to the emergency room.

A few hours later, the ER physician told me that I was "stone-cold normal" and released me to the custody of my friend. I had been dehydrated, hungry, and overheated, but other than a bruised head and a bruised ego, I was fine.

His warning, as I left, was to take better care of myself and to ask for help—just what my universe had been trying to tell me all along. I guess I was just too stubborn to pay attention.

For the next couple of days, I rested. My new facilitators took turns taking care of me while I regained my strength and sense of humor. My best friend stayed faithfully with me night and day. She listened patiently as I rehashed the event and puzzled through the lessons from the fall. All my old buddies and friends called and wished me well.

After that, fresh offers of assistance flooded in from all over. Friends whom I didn't even know I had volunteered their help. My family offered their support. My best friend stepped in as a business partner. My new facilitators shouldered burdens I had carried all alone. It felt awesome to be loved by friends and strangers alike. I was deeply moved by their generosity.

I don't know if my PEACEMAKER Seminars Inc. facilitators decided to make sure I accepted their help, or if it was just a coin-cidence, but from that day forward, I was never without their help, love, and steady support.

I have been given a chance to really grow from this humbling experience. I've turned over a new leaf these days and am entirely more relaxed and peaceful. I use the Peaceful Heart concepts every single day of my life. I balance my work and my play. I avoid toxic situations. I take responsibility for my actions. I allow others to help out when they offer. And I even ask for help. I have faith in the benevolence of the universe.

Since I've started really paying attention to the gentle nudges and more obvious warning signs from my universe, my life has improved on every possible level. It has been the most joyful and exciting year of my entire life.

I'm so glad I fell on my face when I did.

It really got my attention.

I'm happy to say that my beloved PEACEMAKER Seminars Inc. is doing well. We are right where we need to be—in the heartland of America, delivering the one-day Peaceful Heart Seminar wherever and whenever we are asked to do so.

The lesson I learned from my inelegant debut is to pay attention to the neon sign in the sky. Your universe might be trying to tell you something.

It is worth your careful attention, and it just might change or save your life.

Let Us Be of Good Cheer

by Dawn Billings, M.A./LPC

Let Us Be of Good Cheer

by Dawn Billings, M.A./PLC

"Let us be of good cheer, remembering that the misfortunes hardest to bear are those which never happen."

—James Russell Lowell

Edith lay dying in her small, unassuming brick home in Oklahoma. It wasn't large but it was hers, paid for free and clear. Her husband had died over thirty years before. She remembered his death as if it were yesterday. How could she forget? He had died just three days after she had given birth to her fifth baby, on a bare mattress at home. It was a girl.

She named the baby Lily Dawn. Lily, after her husband Tom's mother, and Dawn because they prayed that this new baby's birth would magically create a new beginning in their lives. A new beginning came, but not the one they had prayed for.

It was the middle of the Depression. Things had been hard for everyone, especially Edith and Tom. They had struggled to feed their daughters and keep them clothed. At times they wondered how they would survive, but then it happened. The unimaginable. Edith awoke to cries of hunger from her three-day-old baby girl and found her husband cold and quiet on a cot beside the double bed she was sleeping on. He had died in his sleep. The doctor said that it was a rupture of some kind. It was a rupture all right, a rupture in her heart and in her faith.

Just the night before, her husband, Tom, had calmed her with his quiet words of faith."Don't worry, honey, everything will be just fine," he had assured her.

"Don't worry. Don't worry. What did he mean, don't worry?" she remembered crying to herself all those years ago. She had wanted to believe him. She had forced herself to sleep that night, refusing to worry, and now look where that had gotten her. Confused, angry, and alone, she had wondered: If she had worried, would Tom still be alive? Maybe if she had just worried, her life wouldn't be turned upside down. Maybe. . . . Maybe. . . . Maybe. If only she had worried a little more he might still be alive.

Her husband was taken from their home. The mortuary brought his belongings to her in a small brown paper bag. There wasn't much. An inexpensive pocket watch Tom's father had given him as a wedding present, a worn brown leather wallet that held Tom's identification but no money, and finally, seven cents. That was his legacy: seven cents. That was all he had left her, except for five beautiful daughters. She struggled to be happy with her bounty, but loss and fear were enormous foes. She cried as she realized she was left to raise her children alone.

Edith Hughes was determined. Soaking wet she weighed less than one hundred pounds, and stood all of four feet eleven inches tall. Proudly, she would say that her body may be small, but her will was mighty tall. She was a hard worker, persistent and dedicated. She was strong, but she was never without terror. She was what her friends and family labeled a worrier. After her husband's death she decided that she would never forget to worry again. She had kept that promise, but in these last months of her life, her perspective had changed on many things. When you are diagnosed with cancer, you have time to reflect about life and its many ups and downs and turns. She had time to look through new lenses, and she felt as though she could see more clearly than ever before.

She believed that these breaths that she struggled for were her final ones. She wasn't frightened, which surprised her.

There was a great peace. This peace allowed her to look back at her life with great care and detail and evaluate it. She was surprised by her lack of desire to judge it; instead, she found herself reflecting on her experiences and choices as though they were chapters of some great and fascinating novel. She was interested and eager for deeper understanding. As she reflected on the many hardships of her life, she remembered lying awake so many nights not knowing what or how she was going to feed her daughters the next day. She began to understand that although worry and fear had taken a great toll on her health and stolen many moments of her life, it had never put one slice of bread on her table. She realized that she was afraid of not worrying.

She remembered how she would cry as she cut apart the flour sacks that friends and family saved for her. They would arrive at the old pedal machine as sacks and leave as simple dresses for her girls. For most of her life, she had worried about what they didn't have. Now, she smiled, and joy filled her completely as she remembered what they did have: love, laughter, songs sung in harmony and hope.

She remembered owning only one bed. She wondered now, how in the world she and her five daughters managed to sleep in only one double bed? She smiled, even though at the time it had not been funny. There was pleasure in the memories.

She remembered fighting to be on her own. Her parents had tried to help for the first couple of years after Tom's death, but they were poor crop farmers with extremely limited resources.

Edith remembered, as if it were just yesterday, the day that she was hired for her first job. She would do cleaning at the town nursing home. It paid very little, but she had no skills or experience and was thrilled for the opportunity to take care of herself and her daughters. She was so excited at the thought of being on her own. It was devastating, however, to find that on Wednesday there was no money left from her meager paycheck for food. She did not get paid again until Friday, and her daughter's stomachs were not going to last until then. That was the first time she and her five daughters disassembled the bed and carried it to Mr. Sumpter's pawnshop. She quietly chuckled, as she remembered the image, a petite woman and her five daughters carrying a bed down the street. We must have looked like a line of ducks, she thought to herself. Mr. Sumpter paid her for the bed, and she respectfully requested that he not sell it before Saturday because she planned to buy it back as soon as she was paid. On Friday she and her daughters returned to the pawnshop to pick up their bed.

Mr. Sumpter was a kind man and knew he was doing Edith and her five daughters a great favor by selling their bed back to them for the same price he paid for it two days before. Edith knew that he earned his living by charging more than he paid for the articles in his shop and was humbled by his kind and generous gesture. She shook his hand with a firm and grateful grip, as she turned from sight to wipe her tears. She was a proud woman and hated for anyone to see her cry.

This went on for weeks before Mr. Sumpter could bear the vision of Edith and her daughters carrying the bed to his shop no longer. He told Edith to come by on Wednesdays and he would pay her the money for the bed just as if she had carried it to him. He tried to be stern, as he explained that she could pay back the money on Fridays. He held his face firm, as he informed her that if she did not come on Friday he would come after the bed. He certainly did not want to appear to be less than an astute businessman with a mind for profit. He was not known for his generosity, but in this instance it shined like a full moon on the darkest of nights.

Edith Hughes never failed him. Each Wednesday, for six months, she would arrive like clockwork. And each Friday, rain or shine, her first stop on her way home was Mr. Sumpter's shop to promptly repay him. Finally, Mr. Sumpter suggested that Edith and her girls come to the shop once a week and help him straighten and dust. He explained that he was getting very busy and couldn't keep up with everything by himself. He told her he would pay her the same amount she was accustomed to receiving from him, but she wouldn't have to return on Fridays and pay him back.

Edith never believed that he was too busy. She always believed that some people are put on this earth with their wings hidden under their clothes and Mr. Sumpter, gruff as he attempted to appear, was one of them. The extra money was more of a blessing than Edith could have possibly explained, but somehow, she knew words weren't necessary. She and the girls became quite proficient at the shop and soon were more help than Mr. Sumpter could have ever imagined. After a year or so, Mr. Sumpter hired Edith away from the nursing home by offering her quite a raise. She was a wonderful manager and the girls were always a great help.

Many years later when Mr. Sumpter passed away, Edith remembered her complete surprise when she discovered that Mr. Sumpter had left her the shop and a small rent house that he owned free and clear with a note saying:

You have always treated me with the greatest
appreciation, but now I need you to know,
I did no favor for you and your daughters.
You were the ones who brought favor to my life.
For a small woman, you make quite a mountain.

    With deepest respect,

    Ben Sumpter

"Momma," Betty, Edith's oldest daughter, whispered in her mother's ear, hoping not to startle her.

Oh my goodness, it amazes me how at this time of my life, past and present seem to exist simultaneously. Memories feel as real as the whisper of my daughter's voice in my ear, Edith thought to herself as she struggled to focus.

"We are all here, Mom, just like you requested. What was so important that you wanted to tell us all together?" her daughters asked, attempting to hide their fear of losing their mother.

As Edith opened her eyes wide, attempting to focus clearly, she looked around the bed. She smiled as she recognized five of the most beautiful faces on the planet. Betty, Debbie, Dean, Dorothy, and Little Lily. Lily wasn't little anymore. Edith's daughters had all grown into fine women. She looked deep into the eyes of each daughter as she spoke their names. She was amazed at their common traits and marveled at their differences—each unique, yet, each connected. Oh, how blessed she had been sharing their lives.

"You're all here. Good." Edith struggled to smile and attempted to raise her frail body higher in her bed. Noticing her struggle, her daughters fought for the right to assist her.

"There are things that you know when you reach this phase of your life," she assured her daughters. "One of those things I know is I am the luckiest woman on the face of this earth to have gotten to be your mother. I don't know what I ever did to earn that privilege, but it must have been good. I also know that I haven't got much longer to be here on this earth," she spoke calmly as she tried to maintain her focus.

"It's important that you girls listen close to me at this time. Please pay attention 'cause this may be the most important thing I've told you in your sweet lives," Edith spoke with renewed energy that sometimes comes at the very end of life. She was surprised by the sudden burst of energy and grateful for its timing.

"I am proud of you, every last one of you. You all finished school even though it was hard. Not just the studyin' and such, but the kids makin' fun cause we didn't have much. You all made good decisions about life. You didn't have it easy, but you made my life a pleasure. You gave me a reason—a reason for everything. I worked hard all my life. You all can attest to that, but you worked hard too. You have worked hard on your relationships, cared for your children and loved them good, but most of all you're good people. Maybe that's what I'm most proud of." Edith began to cough and struggled to fill her lungs with air. Her daughters rushed to calm her.

"Just lie still, Momma, and catch your breath," Lily encouraged her, but Edith insisted upon continuing.

"I have learned a great deal in my sixty-four short years. They may be short, but like me, they were each lived tall. Now, more than ever, I want to make sure I leave the important stuff with all of you." Edith's eyes were tired but her inner strength shined bright within them. She weakly coughed and gasped to catch her breath. Her daughters begged her to rest but she was steadfast and determined to finish what she had to say.

"I need you to know that the important stuff isn't the house, the cars, the shop or anything else I may be leaving for you all to split up between you. The important stuff is the love and the knowledge I have to pass on. The love I think you all know and understand, but there is something important that I am afraid that I didn't teach you because it took me a whole lifetime to figure it out myself. Girls . . . ." Edith felt her body failing her. She closed her eyes for just a moment and respect- fully asked for just a few moments more. She felt a calm, her breathing eased and she knew her request had been granted.

"Girls," she continued, "I have had many troubles in my life, troubles so bad that I didn't think I'd survive them. Troubles so terrible they destroyed my health and caused me great pain. The most important thing I want to tell you is most of those troubles I worried about never happened. Pay attention to your dyin' Momma. Listen with your hearts not just your ears. Please, as my last request, don't waste valuable time and energy wor- rying about things that might happen. Fear is a worthless thief, and it wants to steal your peace, your hopes, and your dreams. It has certainly stolen too many of mine. You girls fight back, and don't let it steal yours. Don't let my life, and the lessons that I have learned, be lost. Promise?" Edith's breathing was slow and the time in between was long. Her eyes were closing and opening, slowly dancing in rhythm with her tired lungs.

"Yes Momma, we're listening," the girls whispered as their eyes filled with tears. "We promise."
"It was hard . . . but it was a pleasure . . ." Edith softly spoke her last words of love in a rhythm so gentle and soothing

it sounded like the wind's gentle song of farewell to the sea. "Are you listening?" was her last haunting question.

"Yes Momma," the girls held hands, nodding in agreement, their tears dropping from their cheeks, gently kissing the blanket sheltering their mother. "We're listening and we understand."

With that Edith nodded, gently smiled, surrendered her frail body for wings of freedom, and took her last labored breath.

ॐ

Edith left her daughters secure investments, a small home, a thriving business, and college funds for each of the grandchildren, but nothing she owned had greater value than her last request.

Each day we make choices about how much of our lives will belong to us and how much we are willing to have stolen by worry, fears, and what ifs. What will you choose for your life today?

A Father's Gift

by John Irvin, CSP

A Father's Gift

by John Irvin

It was Christmas day, 1980.

"He's gone," I said to my mother and sister as I came out of the hospital room into the waiting area.

My father was born Raymond William Irvin on May 30, 1909. His mother was Jenny Irvin, originally Jenny Crockett, and his father—well, to tell you the truth, I never even knew his father's name.

My father didn't talk much about his past. I knew that he carried three paper routes when he was in grade school, one in the morning and two after school. I didn't learn until just a couple of years ago that he had never finished high school.

His own father died in 1918, from some kind of rare liver disease. So my father was nine years old and began to help support his family, his mother and younger brother, Wilbur.

Of course in my youth, I never really understood what that meant. I was a child of the '50s, where the modern indulgence of youth began. Oh, sure, I had to pick up my room and mow the lawn. But I certainly didn't have the hardship of having to support a family.

My father owned his own business. He was a mechanic, a garage owner. He had quit his job at an automobile dealership when my mother was pregnant with me. He came home one day at lunch and said that he had quit. "I'm fed up," he said.

My mother was beside herself. She was a child of the depression and she's a natural-born worrier. Imagine the fodder that this would have given her! My goodness, already a five-year-old girl and another child on the way and a husband who is now out of work!

She didn't have to worry long, though. Apparently, before the day was over, people who had learned that my father had quit began showing up at the tiny house my parents rented so that he could do the repairs on their vehicles. My father had a very good reputation, and thus, the birth of Irvin Auto Electric Service.

I was born in February and less than a year later my parents moved into a large house on a two-acre tract in Lincoln Hills, about a four-mile drive from Valparaiso, Indiana.

My father's business prospered, and we lived well. We weren't rich by any means, but we were certainly among the growing middle class. I always had nice clothes, and we always had plenty of food. We had a stereo hi-fi system and I remember when we got a console color TV—one of the first in the neighborhood.

Yes, my dad's business went well. And because of that, I didn't see him much. He got up each day before 7:00 A.M. and was out the door just a few minutes after seven. He would get home at night somewhere between six-thirty and seven. We would have dinner, and he would look at the paper for a bit and then head back out the door to "The Shop," as we called it, until about 9:30 P.M. On Saturdays the shop closed at noon, so he would get home about five or six. Sundays, he was out early and might return somewhere between two and four. It was usually on those weekend days that he would do the manly chores about the house or yard. No, I didn't see him much.

I remember him as being strict. I mean, he didn't seem to be involved with the family much, but when he became involved, you knew he meant business.

Sometimes, my older sister and I would be arguing. He would sit there on the couch, reading the paper and then there would come a point when he would holler out, "Pipe down! Stop it! That's enough!"

We knew it was time to shut up.

It seems like I may have been in the fourth or fifth grade when my father decided that it was time I learned how to work. During my summer vacation, my father would get me out of bed to head in to the shop with him. We would stop for breakfast at the

Big Wheel diner. People always knew him. It seemed like everyone knew him except his own family.

Of course, I was angry. My friends were all in bed and soon they would be getting up and watching some cartoons or going outside to play. And here I was, having to go to work. Good grief! What can a kid do on automobiles? Besides, I didn't even know how to drive!

Well, of course, I got to clean the floor. Yes, there would be big oil or gas stains on the concrete floor and my job was to put down some kind of treated sawdust, rub it into the floor, and then sweep it all up.

The men who worked for my father would bring carburetors to me. I would take them apart and soak the parts in some type of solvent, and then use a brush to scrub each little piece clean. Then I returned them to the one who had given it to me.

I also crawled underneath cars to take off the muffler system that had rusted out. Remember this was in northern Indiana, where they put down some type of salt mixture in the winter time. It's very common for cars to rust because of the salt. I would try to remove the bolts that have been there since the creation of Earth. Rust would fall into my eyes, and the wrench would slip from the bolt. I would bust my knuckles.

Oh, yeah, it was a good time. I hated it!

I would complain. I would whine. I would feign sickness, like some type of migraine headache or severe abdominal cramps. "Please let me go home." I was pathetic, I'm sure.

My father would shake his head in disgust, thinking that I was lazy and wouldn't amount to much.

I began to avoid him, because it seemed that whenever he saw me, there was some job for me to do—a lawn to mow, a hedge to trim, or a floor to sweep.

The summer after I completed the sixth grade, my dad opened a car wash. Yes, an automated ROBO Car Wash. He apparently thought this was the perfect job for a boy during the summer, and when school was in session for Friday night, Saturday and Sunday, noon to six.

We didn't get along, to say the least. I was angry, rebellious and resentful. He was short-tempered, critical and authoritarian. We were the perfect example of a father and son during the late 1960s.

"As long as you're under my roof . . . " he would roar.

So I left home as soon as I could. I graduated high school and moved seven hundred miles away. I was still seventeen at the time.

We had infrequent contact, and when we did, it usually turned into some kind of argument. We were both stubborn and opinionated.

In the fall of 1979, I received word that my father had cancer. It was smoking-related, cancer of the esophagus. He had smoked his entire life. He quit cigarettes in the early 1960s when they were first linked to lung cancer, and he switched to cigars thinking that these were okay since one didn't inhale.

In the spring of 1980, he went to MD Anderson in Houston. They were going to operate. The plan was to remove the cancerous area and replace it with intestine. When they opened him up, however, they found tumors everywhere; he was too far gone. They closed him up, not doing a thing.

A few days before Christmas, I visited my parents, who had moved to Lake Placid, Florida a couple of years before when my father had retired and sold his business. I understood that he wasn't doing well, but living so far away and not being in regular contact, I didn't comprehend the full decay of his being.

My father had always been in tremendous shape. He was not a big man, only about 5'6" in height, and he was slender, very lean, and every ounce of him was muscle. He was strong, active, and vibrant. He was alive!

Now, however, as I walked into the bedroom, I saw a weakened elderly figure lying in the bed. His eyes were closed and he was hooked up to the oxygen tank in the corner of the room. He weighed no more than eighty pounds and looked horrifically comparable to those prisoners from the concentration death camps of World War II.

He lay on the bed gasping for air even as he was hooked up to the oxygen.

I suddenly realized the truth of what was happening. My father was dying.

He opened his eyes briefly and smiled.

"I'm glad you could come," he whispered between gasps.

The room smelled of death.

I sat down in a chair at the foot of the bed and looked in amazement at what was now only a shadow of the vibrant man that once was. A man for whom my only wish had been to be in his good graces, to be someone whom he could be proud of . . . but I had somehow always fallen short of it.

Suddenly, our arguments seemed foolish. We had wasted all those years feeling hurt and anger and fear and resentment, and the reasons didn't seem important anymore.

I sat there through the day and watched him struggle for air.

His frail humanity glared at me and yelled, "Look at me, look! I'm only a man."

He was on quite a bit of morphine at this late stage, and from time to time he would awaken from some type of drug-induced dream. He would cry out, his eyes flying open with a wild look of terror and fear.

My heart began to stir with the compassion that had been missing from our lives and our relationship. Tears came to my eyes. I wept for the love we never shared.

Some time the next morning, he awoke briefly. He looked at me and said again that he was glad that I could make it. I nodded my head.

He gasped for another breath and added, "Listen, I know

we've never gotten along very good." He struggled for the words. "I was doing the best I knew how; I was doing what I thought was right." His effort to tell me those words drained him.

I nodded silently.

"I just want you to know, I love you," he said.

"I know," I said. "I know, it's okay. It's okay."

Later that day, he said he wanted to go to the hospital. An ambulance arrived, and the paramedics transferred him to a stretcher, carried him out and drove to the hospital a few miles down the road. We followed in the car. It was Christmas Eve.

The next day, Christmas, my mother and I had lunch in the hospital cafeteria, dining on turkey, dressing and cranberry sauce. With tears in her eyes, my mother choked a smile, "It's not the best Christmas dinner we've ever had, is it?"

I smiled back and agreed, "No, we've had better."

After lunch, we returned to my father's room.

Later in the day, a nurse came to change the sheets on the bed. My sister and mother left the room while I stayed to help the nurse. As I held my father up and over to one side of the bed, she removed the soiled sheets from that side and replaced them with clean sheets. As she finished that side, we exchanged places. I held my father up and over to the other side of the bed as she finished the bed and then . . . I *felt* it.

My father had silently passed on. I felt the life leave his body. I knew he was gone.

"I think you might want to check him," I suggested to the nurse.

She asked me to wait outside. She closed the drapes around the bed as I stepped into the waiting area.

"He's gone," I said to my mother and sister.

Years have passed now and I know, truly, how fortunate I was to have made that trip to Florida. That Christmas I received the greatest gift I could have possibly experienced. It was truly a gift of the heart.

It was in the dying words of my father, "I was doing what I thought was right. I was doing the best I knew how," that I began to understand one of the greatest truths of our human condition. The power of love and forgiveness. The power of compassion. The truth of faith. We are all on this planet to help one another along the way.

It's an unfortunate fact, though, that none of us are perfect; we falter, we fail, and we hurt one another. And yet, very seldom are those hurts intentional. The person doing the hurting, I truly believe, is not really wanting to hurt us. He or she is just trying to minimize the pain and the suffering that he or she is experiencing, in the hopes of escaping their own pain.

We're all doing the best we can with the knowledge that we have and the tools we possess at that time.

If we can only keep that perspective, we can help to heal our own lives, our own hearts, and we can more fully achieve real positive results.

We know that there are two sets of "attitude activators."

One set is love and faith and hope. The second set is fear and doubt and hate. Each of these two sets of activities cause a clear and distinct set of resulting behaviors and attitudes.

In my workshop, *Bounce Back With A Winning Attitude*, we explore these two sets of activators and the results that are achieved by both, and I want to briefly share them with you here.

When one's primary focus is love, hope and faith, the primary attitudes that spring forth are understanding, anticipation, forgiveness, positive expectations, self-confidence, patience and humility. From these attitudes we witness some uplifting behaviors. We see an enthusiasm and decisiveness develop. We see courage and optimism, cheerfulness and consideration. We see courteousness, sincerity and genuine warmth.

When someone lives his or her life with these attitudes and behaviors, we seem to find, consistently, some very positive results.

What are they? Success, recognition, security, energy, achievement, happiness, growth, adventure, health, friendship, love and inner peace.

But what occurs if our focus is on that second set? Well, then we see the ugly, lonely and horrific side of life. Envy, greed, anger, conceit, cynicism, self-pity, indecision, criticism and inferiority. Not a very pretty picture, is it?

We find inconsideration, pessimism, cruelty, weakness and coldness.

Results? Worry, tension, depression, frustration, weariness, failure, unhappiness, sickness, poverty, loneliness and fatigue.

Where do you want to focus? I know where I want to be.

Faith, hope and love. Forgiveness is a key ingredient.

My first real lesson in this was with my father's dying words. "I was doing the best I knew how."

My heart softened and I realized the pain and resentment we both had. I knew the wasted years of lost relationship and the pain of believing, erroneously, that I was being hurt intentionally. I didn't want to hold onto that any longer.

Healing starts with forgiveness. And I learned to forgive him and myself.

It can be tough, and it may take years. Some of us have experienced terrible trauma and abuse—physical, emotional and sexual—and yet, we must forgive. Perhaps not the deed, but the person, for they have only acted out of their own pain, their own weakness, their own search for truth and fulfillment.

And, the reality is, we don't forgive for their sake, but we forgive for ourselves. Only through forgiveness can we truly experience the faith and hope and love we need in order to achieve our own dreams.

"Father, forgive them, for they know not what they do."

Yes, perhaps that Christmas I received the greatest gift a father could ever give a son.

Three Keys From A Cowboy

by Dr. Michael Johnson

Three Keys From A Cowboy

by Dr. Michael Johnson

Texan by birth,
Cowboy by the grace of God.

Seems I've been learning lessons from cowboys all my life. I'm a Texan by birth and a cowboy by the grace of God. As a young man, I sat in the saddle many hours working alongside and watching my dad and uncles ply their trade. They were rough, tough, macho hombres who rode good horses, and roped like Zen masters shooting a bow. They could do anything with those leathery-thick, sun-bronzed hands. I remember their hands. Those hands could repair a tractor, filet a fish or be so gentle as when helping a mother bring her baby colt into the world. And could they rope! These fellows threw a rope like Mickey Spillane wrote: " . . . clean and to the bone."

I reminisce about those days now. I remember with great fondness the smell of horses, of pecan wood on a campfire and of the sweet aroma of warm alfalfa hay. I close my eyes and can still see redwing blackbirds swaying on cattails, singing repetitious little solos; and momma wood ducks bustlin' around on the pond, tending to their new babies who all looked like fourth-graders just home from the barber shop, complete with fresh flat-tops. The cowboys drank cold beer mixed with tomato juice from icy half-gallon jars, chilled almost to freezing in No. 3 washtubs. All the thick corral dust would be washed down with that frosty elixir, and then they would sit for a time in quiet conversation at the end of a hard day, with good horses and good dogs standing close at hand, tired, but ever-attentive to their master's command. I loved those days then and love them more at this moment so many years later.

Older now, I realize those men offered not only practical day-to-day solutions to ever-pressing ranch problems, but in a much deeper sense, those cowboys practiced behaviors and believed in principles that serve as solid and successful foundations for living a fuller life, on or off the ranch.

While they never held formal classes, still they taught me those principles every day. When I expressed frustration about the work required, one uncle might say, "If it's not in your heart, you won't do it well." When an ornery colt bucked me off, the moment I hit the ground, I would hear, "Happens to all of us, son. Get back up and get back on." If I missed a steer, in an instant I would hear, "Build your loop and throw again . . . try again." Those lessons are still within me, placed there by men who worked a small farm in a remote corner of Texas long ago. Men that I loved and who taught me so much.

Later, when I would fail in life, (and those times would be many) after the requisite period of self-pity, I knew what to do. Because of those lessons, I knew I had to find what was in my heart, brush myself off, get back up and get back on, and keep trying. Sounds sophomoric and simplistic? For much of my early life, I thought so too. But now I know those simple rules are the keys to finding a path of harmony, a path that offers the sweetest of all things . . . the thing called Joy. As has been said, one must gather a handful of mistakes to arrive at something sublime.

In our modern day culture, we rarely, if ever, teach such things any more. Those 'cowboy lessons' seem archaic and out-dated. Our modern day message to youth is something like, "Go to school, work hard and make good grades. Then, get a secure job (with a huge firm) that pays the highest salary possible." While we may not exactly verbalize the message as stated, the underlying suggestion is there. "Everything is predicated on preparing yourself to obtain the best employment position possible . . . and then you will be happy."

Now don't get me wrong. I certainly believe in education, making good grades and working hard. I was hard on myself about those things and on my own kids as well. Naturally, we should go to school, become educated and do our best. It's just the last part that bothers me " . . . and then you will be happy."

At the university where I teach, at least once a week some well-meaning student comes in and asks if he or she might talk about career choices. I know what the question will be. The question is always the same. "What kind of good job can I get that pays the most money?"

When I was a younger man, I would try to talk to that student at length about a more productive path for finding one's life's work. Now, I just jump on them and start choking . . . okay, I'm kidding!

Students do, however, sense my irritation and ask, "What's wrong with that question? Isn't that the American dream?"

"Yes, I suppose it is," I sigh, "but here is the source of my frustration. Your approach to finding your path, that is, the journey you will take in life is a weak and ineffectual one. To prove my point, I am going to ask you some questions, and you will not be able to answer a single one of them. Ready?"

"Certainly," replies the student, confident that lifetime employment is only a few answers away.

"Very well then, you say you want a good job that pays a lot of money, correct?"

"Correct," says Mr. Every Student.

"My first question, then, is, 'What is a good job?' "

At this point, there will be a blank look, some confusion and a good deal of muttering, followed at last by, "Well, I don't know." (See, I told you he wouldn't know.) "A good job would be one that pays a lot of money, I guess."

"Great, now we're rolling," I respond. "Second question, what would you consider a lot of money?"

More muttering, more confusion, followed by, "Well, gee, I don't know." (See?) "Not a lot, but enough. You know . . . enough to do what I want to do."

"Fine, what is it that you want to do? "

"I don't know," the student will say in exasperation, "It all depends on whether I can get a good job or not! That's why I'm in here talking to you!"

Can you see how lost that person is? And I'm afraid to say it, but we taught him to ask those very questions. That philosophy of 'getting a good job that pays the most money' is so weak you can't even get a burger in a fast food restaurant with it.

Try it.

Go to your favorite hamburger joint and when the attendant asks, "What would you like?" say something like, "Well, gee, uh . . . I'm not sure, depends on what you have. Something good, not too much, but you know, I want to be filled up."

Looking very nervous now because of your bizarre behavior, the attendant will say, "Well, there are many choices. What is it that you want?"

Would your response be, "I'm just not sure. It all depends on what I can get"?

Isn't that the height of absurdity? Yet, that is exactly what so many of us do with our lives. We wait on that deal, that job offer, or the winds of fate to come along and set us off on the right course. Hey, weak method! We have to make it happen. They didn't come looking for Elvis or Garth Brooks. It's unlikely that they have a talent squad frantically searching for you and me.

While I certainly believe the Spirit works in our lives, and also believe in the thing called serendipity, what parent doesn't like it if the child offers to help? There is no doubt in my mind that the Lord helps us, but surely He must be pleased if we get off our butt and help ourselves, just as we are most appreciative when our own children do the same.

The answer to that student's dilemma, and for most of us, is to remember what my uncles said about work," If your heart's not in it, you won't do it well."

Simple words that we all already know, right? I wonder. Do most of us really live our lives pursuing the thing inside that calls to us? Or do we look at career choices with a more logical eye and consider retirement, insurance, and 401K plans as key determinants of how we will live? So many of us choose that latter safer path; these are the easily recognized ones Thoreau spoke of . . . (those leading lives of quiet desperation.) Here is a far superior method in terms of career choice and a path to success.

Key number one: Find your passion.

No better advice can be found than that of mythology scholar, Joseph Campbell, who advised, "Follow your bliss." Do the thing you love and would do for free . . . and find a way to get someone to pay you for doing it.

Many would object to such advice and call me an LSD hippie. Not so—I'm a washed-up calf-roper from Oklahoma. However, after fifty-four years on this earth, a doctorate in psych and lots of rodeos, I have become convinced the primary key to living a more fulfilled life is to find that dream, desire, vision, quest or purpose placed inside you by something more than all of us.

Don't say it isn't in there. It's in there. Your task on this earth is to find it and share it with others. Shaw said, "The most grand and noble thing we can do is discover our purpose." Not your job, not your career, but your work. That is what we should teach our children and ourselves.

Once we discover that purpose, the oddest thing happens. The opaque fog lifts just a bit. Now, I didn't say on a clear day, you can suddenly see forever, but visibility does improve significantly. And that passion and purpose will sustain you during your darkest days. Like my old uncle said, "If your heart's not in it, you won't do it well." And most importantly, once you have found your path, the resultant strength you will acquire from being on that path will prepare you for Key number two.

Key number two: Handle failure and rejection.

Whenever one of those young colts caused me to have a sudden meeting with the ground, one of my cowboy uncles would quietly say, "Happens to us all, son. Get back up and get back on." 'Course at the time, I didn't want to. Hurt too bad. All the wind was knocked out of me, and I just didn't think I could go on. But you know what?

I have learned something.

We are stronger than we think we are. We are stronger than we know.

Shaw also said, "If you live long enough, everything happens to you." Death, divorce, loss of loved ones, jobs disappear, homes destroyed, and the list goes on and on . . . . Things will happen, and we find ourselves at the bottom of the universe.

How can we continue?

Well, while I don't mean to make light of tragedy because some pain is so very difficult to bear, it helps to keep a couple of things in mind. First, when you're in a valley, remember that old saw about peaks on either side. Remember things will not always be this way. If life stayed the same rotten way, I would agree that perhaps we need to check out permanently. Fact is, however, things will not stay the same. Sounds trite, but all cliches are true . . . . This too shall pass.

Second, I find great strength in John 1:5, "In the darkness, there is light." When you are on that valley floor, try to remember there is wisdom lying all around you. Even though we can't see it at the moment, (too many teardrops?) later, we will realize all that we have gained because of the experience. We really never learn anything that truly helps us when things are going well. It's only when we get the living hell kicked out of us—and live through it— that we become more of what we can be. (I don't particularly like that rule, but that's the way it is.)

On a lighter note, when you discover that passion and become obsessed with your newfound direction, get ready for the big 'deflation.' Get ready for rejection.

Not from CEOs, or editors, or deans of universities, but from family members, friends, former teachers and spouses. The people closest to you will shake their heads with a simpering little smile on their face and say your name two or three times like you are such an idiot. Then they will explain how you have always been a dreamer, never had a practical bone in your body and point out all your other failures. Then, in their wisest old-fogey voice, they will explain how others have gone broke doing this same thing, how the big boys have it all sewn up, and how you just cannot possibly compete. And your spirit is crushed. Get over it. I have a little phrase I use to cope with these prophets of gloom and doom, and you can use it too. Here it is . . . to hell with 'em.

See folks, there are really only two kinds of people on the planet. There are givers and takers. All takers will tell you that you can't, and in the process they get to feel superior. (For some reason, when we encounter these negative energy drainers, we forget they have never done a damn thing.)

On the other hand, there are givers. These are beings that look like ordinary humans, but in reality, they are much more. They give of themselves with encouragement, facts, wisdom and empowerment. Here is what you do: Look for the givers; surround yourself with them and be like them. Cut yourself loose from the takers. The two most common things in the universe are hydrogen molecules and horses' butts. Don't be either one, and don't let either one bother you.

A woman in Michigan, who was a big-time publisher, (according to her) told me no one would read my 'sappy stories' about teachers, and she really ripped my tale about my beloved roping horse, Susie. Now several years later, either several thousand people who bought *The Most Special Person and Susie, The Whispering Horse* were stupid, or the woman in Michigan was. You decide.

People laughed Freud off the stage when he presented his first paper in Vienna. Kurt Vonnegut was kicked out of the University of Chicago. A record exec told Elvis to get a job driving a truck because he lacked talent. Michael Jordan's high school principal told him to join the Air Force because he just didn't have the skills for basketball. And then, there is this other fellow I really admire, who was told countless times about having no talent, no ability and that he should give up his dream . . . he became World Champion Bull-Rider, Tuff Hedeman.

Yep, it's a fact. When you devote yourself to your dream, you will get bucked off, and it will hurt. Just remember . . . handle that rejection. Like cowboys say, "Happens to all of us. Get back up and get back on."

And if anybody says you can't, to hell with 'em.

Key number three: Learn the Greatest Secret.

Whenever I missed a steer with my rope, my uncle would immediately say, "Coil your loop and throw again. Try again." If I asked, "What did I do wrong, why did I miss?" he would always respond, "You haven't thrown your loop enough."

And that, my friends, is the greatest secret. Here it is . . . .

The Master in His wisdom puts a double dose of the ability to try again in all of us . . . if we just choose to remember that we have it.

Let me tell you about someone who learned that lesson well. When my daughter was a little girl, she decided she wanted to be something special at her school. I asked, "What is it that you want?"

She thought for a time and answered, "I want an award. I want to be a cheerleader, or first chair in band, or win something in a beauty contest."

That was the first time I told her about the great secret. We memorized that little verse together. The Master in His Wisdom puts a double dose of the ability to try again in all of us . . . if we just choose to remember that we have it. My daughter was about ten and she looked up at me and said, "I will always remember." And she began her quest . . . and it was a disaster.

This poor kid failed at every turn. At first, I would encourage her and tell her not to worry. She would always say, "Don't worry, Dad, I will be fine. I have a double dose of try in me." And it got worse.

When she was in the sixth grade, I would sit in the audience watching her in a beauty pageant. I would silently plead, "Lord, let her win a fourth, let her win Miss Congeniality—anything that we could go home and celebrate." Nothing. No first chair in band, no cheerleader, no majorette, no nothing for eight years. Talk about a drought. Through it all, she held her head high and would always say, "I have a double dose of try in me. All I have to do is remember that I have it."

And it started to wear on me.

One night, I was working in the garage and she walked by me. She was in her senior year now, and I was so proud of her. She never gave me any trouble, made good grades, and everything seemed fine, except for that one dream. She had never received an award.

"Where are you going, Dear?" I asked.

"I'm going to the band hall, Dad," she answered. "I'm going to try out for Drum Major."

My heart sank. I wanted to say, "Terre, they are not going to let you be the Drum Major. You have never been first chair, never been a majorette, and they certainly won't let you have this highest honor." But I didn't say that.

She thought I was going to say something else. She said, "I know, Dad. I'll be fine. I remember the verse. I have a double dose of try in me." And she got in her car and drove away. And I got really mad.

I was mad at all the silly rules we have that make others feel left out. Mad at a system that didn't see a young woman's real beauty and hard work. Most of all, I was irrationally mad at my daughter. I wanted to chase her down, open her car door and yell at her, "Stop doing this! You are killing yourself and killing me. If they don't see how good you are, it's their problem!" But I didn't do that.

You know the feeling. When your child is hurting, you would do anything to take the pain, but in this case, I couldn't. I wanted to get really drunk. That didn't seem too wise a course, so I didn't do that either. I went to bed about 9:30 with a heavy heart.

At exactly 10:30 P.M., a BOOM awakened me! It was my backdoor slamming. Then I heard a series of smaller boom–boom–boom–booms . . . her feet running down the hall. My daughter hit my bedroom door with full force and landed some ten feet in the middle of the room.

"Daddy, I got it!" I will never forget those words or that moment until long after I'm dead.

"You did?" I asked, sitting up in the bed, trying to hide my amazement. "Tell me about it," I said, wondering if this was all a dream.

"The band director," she began breathlessly, "when all the tryouts were finished, he said, 'Well, some of you have more talent than others, some have more coordination, but there is one . . . .'" At this point, her eyes filled with tears.

"Dad, he said there was one he had been watching all her life. And this one always got up when she failed. He said she always tried again. Then, he said, 'That's the kind of person we need to lead the band and to lead us in life.' Then, he said, 'Terre is the new Drum Major.' I got it Dad, I finally won."

And like all parents do in such situations, I took complete and total credit for the victory. I said, "Well, it's about time you finally started listening to me. I told you that you could do it. See, it's just a matter of believing."

We then proceeded to the middle of the bed and had a world-class pillow fight 'til the wee hours of the morning and knew the thing called Joy. And standing in feathers a foot deep, the victory was made so much sweeter by all those dark times and all those failures.

If you ever see my daughter, who is now very successful, please don't tell her I gave up the faith for a moment, because she still thinks I'm a hero. Of course, you and I know she is the hero. People who fight the good fight, keep the faith and finish the race are always the heroes.

The good news is we can all be one. By concentrating on a few simple keys learned from old cowboys long ago, we can do it too. Find what's in your heart, handle the inevitable rejections, and when you miss, throw your loop again. That's always the problem . . . you just haven't thrown your loop enough. And if anyone says you can't, to hell with 'em.

Trophies Of The Heart

by Rhett Laubach

Trophies Of The Heart

by Rhett Laubach

Casey Kennedy, my professional speaking partner, and I were in Jefferson City, Missouri, in March of 2000 conducting a youth leadership conference for the Missouri FCCLA (Family, Career and Community Leaders of America). Each morning, over 150 students and teachers would enjoy breakfast at the hotel's restaurant. Monday morning, the manager was not expecting to be rushed by so many people. She was frazzled, frustrated and definitely not in a friendly mood! Every chance I get during my travels, I give "You Rule" recognition cards to certain people I believe deserve either a thank you or a note of encouragement. At the end of the first morning rush, I slipped one of these cards into the pocket of the restaurant manager. I wrote on the card, "Thank you for getting our students ready for the day with a good breakfast."

Tuesday, Wednesday and Thursday mornings she came into the restaurant looking like a million dollars with a billion-dollar smile and a trillion-dollar personality! She was beaming; she was doing her job better; she was making the lives of those around her better; and, as an added bonus, she thought Casey and I "walked on water." She got us anything and everything we needed the rest of the week. Although that wasn't the purpose of the note, it certainly helped tremendously to have a friend on the inside at that hotel!

In my ten years of studying and teaching leadership and life skills, I have learned a truly amazing quality of life is born from appreciating others, and this appreciation leads to an abundance of trophies of the heart.

What Are Trophies of the Heart?

Trophies of the heart are intangible rewards for developing tangible relationships and results. These trophies are prizes you receive without the intention of receiving. They cannot be bought, sold, borrowed or destroyed. They can only be born out of acts of the heart, and the heart is where they will always return. A truly amazing quality of life is achieved not by amassing great wealth but rather a great store of trophies of the heart. The key strategy is to give trophies to others on a regular, consistent basis and help people build their stockpiles, as well!

The Basics

Let's begin by painting a clear picture of what basics must be present in order to accomplish anything, let alone a truly amazing quality of life. In the summer of 2000, I studied the sport of running and found some simple "achievement principles" in the lifestyle of runners.

Jack Wing, an avid runner, says the most common quality found in runners is professional and personal success. Wing says, "Motivation to succeed in life is very common in avid runners." Daniel Goleman, Ph.D., author of *Working with Emotional Intelligence*, defines motivation as "a competency we use to move and guide us toward our goals, to help us take initiative and strive to improve." Dr. Goleman focuses on three main motivational competencies that correlate directly to the motives of runners.

First, runners have a strong drive to achieve. They are action-oriented people. Larry Raynes, a runner of fourteen years and owner of Bestyet Foods in Perry, Oklahoma, states, "It is a great source of achievement for me. I run competitively, but I am mostly in competition with myself. I keep a journal and score myself based on how successfully I achieve my daily and weekly goals, very much like I do with my business."

Second, runners enjoy the price of commitment to a task. They make sacrifices to meet their long-term goals. Dr. Julie Ness, a consultant for SourceSpeakers.com, says there are as many different motives for runners as there are types of sports. However, Dr. Ness identified a few commonalities: "Runners enjoy what they do. They have learned to love running and therefore make a commitment to their exercise schedule just as they would a business meeting."

Third, they are skilled optimists. Runners operate from hope of success rather than fear of failure. They put this skill to work most effectively through positive self-talk. Dr. Ness explains: "Many people do not exercise simply because they talk themselves out of it. Either it is too hot, too cold, or they do not have enough time, etc. When you do not feel like performing a task, an effective technique is to focus on your purpose for the activity instead of the barriers stopping you."

A truly amazing quality of life takes a dedicated effort and is not achieved overnight. Walk into any bookstore in America and you will find hundreds of books, just like this one, designed to help you or advise you in some form or fashion. There are many differences in philosophies and there are many similarities. It has been my experience that these three basics are among those similarities. Study them, learn them, and apply them in your life on a daily basis in the areas covered in the following sections. Owning a desire to achieve, staying committed to your goals, and practicing optimism will help guide you in your journey of giving and receiving trophies of the heart.

How Do I Know I Need to Work on My Quality of Life?

1. I never seem to have enough energy to just get through the day, let alone operate at my best.

2. My temper has a very short fuse.

3. I can never find the positive in challenging people or situations.

4. I find myself constantly defending my actions and words.

5. I look for and highlight people's mistakes and misfortunes.

6. I have not moved one inch closer to personal or professional dreams or goals.

7. My relationships do not bring me joy.

8. I cannot break unhealthy habits, and I let them control my emotions and actions.

9. I always blame other people or "unfortunate circumstances of my life" for my failure to achieve my dreams or goals.

10. I am doing nothing in my life to learn more about or improve my relationships, my work, my faith or myself!

What Are My Trophies?

Make three columns on a piece of paper. Title the first "Happy," the second "Today," and the third "Goals." In the first column, list everything that makes you happy (people, places, tasks, hobbies, etc.). In the second column, list everything you do during an average day. Finally, in the third column; list your personal and professional goals. Now, circle the items that are present in all three columns. This is a great starter list for recognizing your trophies of the heart.

The Friendship Trophy

I have two quick suggestions on how to improve your quality of life by developing more meaningful personal and business friendships. First, help others be their best every day and expect nothing in return. Second, offer constructive criticism only when you are able to give a positive offering. What I am asking you to do is to be an improver instead of a disapprover.

In October of 2000, I facilitated a six-hour brainstorming session with the student organization leaders of Republic High School in Republic, Missouri. Our purpose was to develop a community service project that all the organizations could work on together. It was an awesome experience and a great idea!

After four hours the students voted to remodel and re-open their run-down city park. Two seconds after the vote was cast, the negative talk started. "We've tried this before." "We will never get this accomplished while we are in high school." "There are too many local and state regulations." "The city will never cooperate."

The next hour was filled with a crystal clear picture of what really kills or energizes the enthusiasm in ideas and people— disapprovers and improvers. The students focusing only on the negatives and the reasons why the idea was bad were acting as disapprovers. Those students who chose to view the negatives as challenges and focus more on the positives were acting as improvers.

With a little persistence (and a guiding hand from the facilitator), the improvers outweighed the disapprovers and the disapprovers agreed to get behind the idea and work together to accomplish the common goal. The students were left with two thoughts. First, the park idea is a good or a bad one based solely on whether they think it is good or bad. Their approach in thinking defines the situation. Second, the quality of their effort as a school in completing the project will be based in large part on how effectively the disapprovers can get as passionately behind the idea as they were able to get so passionately against it.

This approach works the same way with your network of friends. Make the good choice to be an improver. Believe me, this world has enough disapprovers already!

The friendship trophy is certainly a two-way street. The support system I enjoy with a few select friends is invaluable. One in particular is the ten-year friendship I have enjoyed with the inventor of P.B. Slices, Stewart Kennedy. (P.B. Slices are creamy, individually wrapped peanut butter slices available at your local grocery store.) Stewart has asked me to help him identify the market demand and penetrate those markets. Stewart is also a professional speaker, and we started YourNextSpeaker.com together in 1998. Both of these business ventures have taken our personal friendship to a new level because we are available to each other for support and advice.

This friendship has improved my quality of life by providing numerous opportunities to give and receive trophies of the heart. Many people are not realizing their great, awesome, God-given potential because they do not have enough people giving them the proper amount of support and encouragement to do so. Friendships are gifts from God, and they play a vital role in creating your own truly amazing quality of life.

The Family Trophy

Growing up in rural Oklahoma, I was surrounded by many other loving family members every day. Anything good I have in me started from my parents' active and present love for each other and our family. Their ability and willingness to share this love has been one of my most treasured trophies. However, my definition of family was very traditional. Today my definition is much broader and has allowed me to make a more positive, significant contribution to society. Let me explain.

In 1984 three men quit their high-paying jobs and moved to the city where their dying mother lived. In Phoenix, Arizona, a daughter gave her father a kidney and saved his life. Every Sunday a young man visits his grandparents for supper and conversation. On any given day this month, a brother will go out of his way to take extra care of his younger sibling. These are stories of people who understand the importance of protecting and serving your family first.

Let's look a little deeper at the concept of family.

In Omaha, Nebraska, a man approaches an inept father who has been verbally abusing his own daughters. For six years, a woman has been meeting a battered wife for coffee and counseling. Next week another boy will have a positive, real-life (not MTV or Universal Studio) male role model when his Big Brother arrives for their meeting. These people are taking their vision of the word "family" to the next level and applying help wherever a "family" need arises.

I believe the cure to this nation's moral and ethical dilemmas is complex, but the best start is simple—take care of the family on a personal and community level. The daily application of this solution is spending time to help whoever needs to improve their mind, body, spirit and soul until they feel like "family."

As I travel the country speaking to thousands of young people, I see a great need for functional families to reach out to non-functional ones. So many of our families lead lifestyles that are breeding grounds for contempt, disrespect, communication deficiencies because of a lack of discipline, attention and love. Every day after my character/positive life skills presentations, students who live in these environments approach me with questions, confusions, heartache, fear, pain and misunderstandings.

These young people are missing an important part of their life skills education because their school is focused on traditional academics, and their family cannot teach what they do not know.

I believe it is time we invest more time in understanding and creating new solutions for not only our own personal family matters, but also situations in our community where we are aware of a fundamental breakdown in the family. I believe it is time to take this responsibility and put it in the hands of the community on a mass, grassroots scale.

Does this mean sticking your neck out? Yes! Does this mean adding to your daily "To Do" list? Yes! Does this mean accepting a broader vision of the meaning of the word "family"? Yes! Will these steps move you closer to a truly amazing quality of life? Yes!

The Professional Achievement Trophy

A recent study of the U.S. working population indicated that 26% were engaged in their work, 55% not engaged, and 19% actively disengaged. These numbers are startling when you think about the unbelievably low level of productivity occurring due to people's general lack of interest in their work. I challenge you to be part of the 26% who are actively engaged by being an innovator in the workplace. Be the person who is asked to tackle the challenges no one else is socially, emotionally or intellectually developed to handle and conquer. How do you do that? Have passion, get intense or get out! This does not mean, be a hard case. It does mean, care enough and take enough pride in your work and yourself to put more in than is expected of you. If you really want to be appreciated at work, you must work smarter and with more passion, go beyond the call of duty, do the dirt jobs, put up with a certain amount of unfair practices and situations, be flexible, and, if it's not working out, be strong enough to get out! Basically, put your heart into it and trust that you will be rewarded!

If you have the misconception that your job doesn't require you to be creative or passionate, consider Paul's situation. Paul works as a tollbooth collector on the New Jersey Turnpike near New York City. His job would seem very mundane and very passive. Just take the money and give the change. Nothing to get excited about, right? Wrong! When five people are in the line next to Paul's booth, twenty are in Paul's. This is because people who travel that toll road on a consistent basis go out of their way to get in Paul's line. They will actually wait an extra ten minutes just to see Paul. This happens because people are attracted to Paul's extraordinary attitude and pleasant manners. He goes out of his way to stay positive and give compliments freely.

Paul has taken a very demotivating work environment and turned it into one that changes the attitude of everyone he serves. You can do the same. With creativity, a commitment to your work, and an appreciative attitude, you will be miles closer to a truly amazing quality of life through the regular practice of receiving and, more importantly, giving trophies of the heart.

The Personal Accomplishment Trophy

Everyone's viewpoint of personal accomplishment is different. What is "just OK" to one person is awesome to another. What is ambitious and creative to me might be barely acceptable to you. Therefore, a discussion about accomplishment must be somewhat generalized. However, I have seen hundreds of individuals who I know are not enjoying a truly amazing quality of life. These people have grown relaxed and filled with apathy. They just don't care. These are the people who, if seated in one of my seminars, would have their arms crossed saying, "Don't try to motivate me. I'm cool right where I am." They are satisfied with trying to get as much as they can with the least amount of effort. I believe in and endorse working less by working smarter, but not working less simply because you think there is no reason to work harder.

I challenge you to make the tough and unpopular choice of being a person who acknowledges that you have room for growth or improvement. When you are green, you are growing. When you are ripe, you are rotting.

This journey toward a truly amazing quality of life, one filled with trophies of the heart, is separated into four stages.

The first stage is Getting By. In this stage, you are just struggling to make a change in your life or deal with an expected change. Moving past this stage takes hard work, learning from past failures and trying again. It takes heart. You have to be passionate about what you really want, why you want it, and how making this change will help you create a truly amazing quality of life.

The second stage is Getting Comfortable. This stage is a "leveling off" of sorts. Many people stop at this stage of development because of the Chicken Littles in their life. Chicken Littles are those people who brighten the room when they leave. They are only there to point out the negative. Chicken Littles are small people with small brains and small hearts doing small things with their small lives. If you don't want to not have criticism in your life, do nothing—say nothing—be nothing. If you want to move past the Getting Comfortable stage, do not believe the Chicken Littles of the world—believe what's in your heart. Listen to your heart!

The third stage is Getting Rewarded. This is where you really feel like positive change is happening. To reach this stage, you must develop your own definition of success and stay committed to it. Never blindly accept the worldview or others' personal views of success—create your own. Obviously, if you are going to reach a certain milestone in your life, you first have to identify and stay focused on it.

If you work hard, learn from your mistakes, believe in yourself, and define what success means to you, you will reach **the fourth stage—Giving Back.** At this stage you have reached significance in your life. You have overcome your fear and worked hard to accomplish something tangible. You are now ready to help others do the same by focusing on giving trophies of the heart. The best part of the deal is that by giving, you will receive more than you could have ever imagined.

If you are ready to create more trophies of personal accomplishment, get out a blank sheet of paper. Think of just one part of your life you want to improve and write down the following items:

1. One part of your life you want to improve.

2. A realistic deadline date to measure your improvement and/or accomplish your goal.

3. Three benefits of making this change.

4. Three negatives of not making this change.

5. Three people to tell about this desired change to help and/or encourage you.

6. One person who has made a similar resolution, to serve in a resource and inspiration capacity.

7. One thing you can do every day to move towards improvement.

8. One thing you need to take away from your daily routine to make room in your life for this improvement.

9. How you will feel when you make this improvement.

Now sign it, hang it up where you and others will see it every day; get after it; watch the personal accomplishment trophies start to roll in, and feel the warm blanket of a truly amazing quality of life!

The Constructor Trophy

You could also call this the "Random Acts of Kindness" Trophy or the "Just a Good, Solid, Nice Person" Trophy. A Constructor makes conscious decisions every day to be a part of the solution, not a part of the problem. Constructors operate from a service-oriented frame of mind, set of values and core beliefs. The core principle influencing their decision to be a Constructor is a belief that it is their responsibility to help fellow human beings improve. Being a Constructor holds real value and substantial significance in their own lives and in the lives of the people they help build on a daily basis. Taken to the grandest and most involved level, the actions of Constructors reach beyond you and me and touch our communities, our nation and our world.

So, what do you do when it seems the people you are trying to help do not appreciate you or just simply do not want your help? The following is your answer:

People are unreasonable, illogical and self-centered. Love them anyway!

If you do good, people will accuse you of selfish, ulterior motives. Do good anyway!

If you are successful, you will win false friends and true enemies. Succeed anyway!

The good you do today will be forgotten tomorrow. Do good anyway!

Honesty and frankness make you vulnerable. Be honest anyway!

The smallest person with the smallest mind can shoot down the biggest person with the biggest ideas. Think big anyway!

What you spend years building may be destroyed overnight. Build anyway!

People really need help but may attack if you help them. Help people anyway!

Give the world the best you have and you might get kicked in the teeth. Give the world the best you have anyway!

Treasure Your Trophies

In April of 2000, I was moving from Stillwater, Oklahoma to Tulsa. My wife, Ashley, best friend Jason Rogers, and I loaded the last of my things and left during a huge thunderstorm for Tulsa. The driving conditions were terrible. The rain was coming down so hard many people were pulling over and waiting for it to subside. In this particular stretch of road, the turnpike's median was grass and only 15 feet wide. A car in the oncoming traffic started to swerve back and forth. It started spinning, jumped the median, continued to spin across our two lanes, went through the ditch, and finally stopped in an open field. When the car jumped the median, it missed our back bumper by only a few feet.

Jason was following behind us and the car missed him by only five car lengths. We were filled with fear, then relief, and then an enormous resurfacing of our appreciation of life. We were thankful just to be alive!

Anyone who has been involved in a near-miss accident understands how much it affects your thinking and how much more thankful you are for all the wonderful trophies God puts in your life. I challenge you to take time to consider what and whom you are most thankful for in your life. Then take time to let them know. You never know if you will have another chance!

Also, if you are going to create a truly amazing quality of life for yourself and your family, you must find and appreciate the amazing elements of your life today. Just because there is room for improvement does not mean your life is totally void of anything good today. Find the positive people and situations in your life and use their strength to empower your dreams. She who finds nothing good in today will find only the same tomorrow.

The King's Highway

Once a king had a great highway built for the members of his kingdom. After it was completed, but before it was opened to the public, the king decided to have a contest. He invited as many as desired to participate. Their challenge was to see who could travel the highway the best and the reward would be great.

On the day of the contest, the people came in their finest chariots, clothing and jewelry. People traveled the highway all day. However, each one complained to the king of a large pile of rocks and debris in the road. They all had to travel around it to reach their destination.

At the end of the day, a lone traveler crossed the finish line wearily and walked over to the king. He was tired and dirty, but he addressed the king with great respect and handed him a bag of gold. He explained, "I stopped along the way to clear a pile of rocks and debris that was blocking the road. This bag of gold was under it all. This is your highway and your pile of rocks. The gold must be yours, as well. I came to return it to its rightful owner."

The king replied, "You are the rightful owner."

The traveler looked up, "Oh, no! This is not mine. I've never known such money."

"Oh, yes," said the king, "you've earned this gold. You have won my contest. You see, he who travels the road best is he who makes the road smoother for those who will follow."

The road in this story symbolizes your life, the rock pile is a hardship, fear or challenge in your life, and the gold bag is a stockpile of trophies of the heart. Dig down deep and find the heart to face the rock pile instead of going around it! It will take much from you, but it will give so much more in return.

Good luck with your journey, treasure your trophies, and enjoy your truly amazing quality of life. Let me know if I can help you along the way!

Dream Weaver: The Shadows In Our Mind?

The Dream Was Not The Answer, It Was The Question!

by Jeff Magee, Ph.D., PDM, CSP, CMC

Dream Weaver: The Shadows In Our Mind?

The Dream Was Not The Answer, It Was The Question!

by Jeff Magee, Ph.D., PDM, CSP, CMC

With each heartbeat, the veins in his head pulsated. Within minutes, sweat beads rolled down the forehead and his eyes swelled up with tears as his vision became blurred!

These pounding headaches were becoming more and more common as he entered high school, and the pain could no longer be controlled or kept a secret from others.

Being a smaller–statured child than most of his peers and an introvert in personality, he became an easy target for the other students in a big city school to single out or ignore altogether. Even when he tried to fit in by participating in athletics, it seemed that extreme physical activity aggravated the headaches.

These activities would stimulate headaches so severe that they would always end with violent vomiting and exhaustion so strenuous as to render him unconscious into a deep sleep.

During his unconscious state, he could make out faint images through his blurred vision. It was difficult to distinguish actual details and determine precisely what he was seeing.

As the headaches became ever more pronounced, the need to determine the cause became paramount. Some of the best medical minds were convinced that the solution lay within the science of medicine. The path became clear as doctors were consulted, in respect to what one should do to determine the causes of the 'migraine headaches.'

First, there were the blood tests and the probing medical

hands. No answers! Then there were the EEG and EKG tests. No answers! Then there were the various x-rays. No answers!

All the while, the sweat beads perspired down from the veins on his forehead and his eyes swelled up with water. His vision became blurred and with each heartbeat you could see the veins in his head pulsate!

The best medical minds were even more perplexed now. They had failed to find a cause.

The latest in medical technology was the CAT scan and a session was hurriedly scheduled for the boy.

The boy was injected with a dye medicine in preparation for the scanning. In the process of the scan, there was an adverse reaction to the injection, and his face and head swelled up beyond recognition. The boy was rushed to the emergency room where the doctors quickly determined that he was merely having a reaction to the injection and that the reaction was not life threatening. To counter the swelling which had distorted his face and to reduce the headache pain, he was given a second shot which induced drowsiness.

The boy quickly fell into a sleep that lasted for two days. When he awakened, not only did he have no recollection of what had happened, he didn't realize he had slept for 48 hours!

So, too, went this latest endeavor with no answer! The parents and doctors became nervous that there were no evidence or answers were being revealed from their best resources.

So the next plan of action was to initiate physical therapy treatments every other morning. At 6:00 A.M. every other day, the boy arrived at the hospital with his parents to undergo heat therapy on the base of his neck, in an attempt to reduce tension within the muscles and reduce stress within the body. For a while, the headaches subsided and so too did the pain.

Just as everyone felt they had arrived at a solution, the headaches returned with even greater vigor. What was thought to be the answer was in fact, no answer!

The more that everyone focused on possible answers to the very real problem and focused on previously detected solutions to similar types of headaches, the further it appeared to everyone to be the answer to this situation.

As the best medical minds and the boy's parents continued their search, three new options were offered: First, undergo exploratory brain surgery; second, seek chiropractic treatments; and, third, invest time with a psychiatrist to determine possible mental causes.

In a passionate plea, one doctor commented that mainstream medicine at that time did not really acknowledge chiropractic or psychiatric professionals in the same line as traditional medical doctors, and before he would pursue the exploratory brain surgery on this child, he would first exhaust all other options.

And with that, the parents pursued at the same time both the chiropractic treatments and psychiatric treatments.

While the chiropractic treatments did reduce the occurrence and amount of pain the headaches created, they did not eliminate them. In fact, there would still be occurrences of headaches so painful that the violent vomiting would return from time to time; his eyes would tear up and crying would only worsen the pain!

So chiropractics too would prove not to be the answer!

When the boy and psychiatrist met for the first time the boy felt too intimidated to share his inner feelings and talk about his family and friends with a stranger. Once the two began talking and they developed a healthy dialogue, it became evident that this interaction had more potential than with previous doctors. First, answers were not the focus. Instead, questions were the focus!

Stop Looking For Answers and Start Asking

The Hard Questions First . . . Answers Will Always

Reveal Themselves!

The approach this time be not to find a solution or even to measure this problem against previous solutions but to retract and explore questions that may make the answer or solution obvious. The boy became hopeful at this promising new perspective.

The psychiatrist asked what was happening each time previous to the headaches. The one consistency is every time there was a bad headache sequence, there had been either a frightening dream the night before or in the nights pursuant to the headaches. The more frightening the dream, the greater the pulsating veins on the head and the deeper the headache pain.

The Dream Was Not The Answer,

It Was The Question, Which When Identified,

Led To The Answer!

As they explored the dream sequence, they reached a cor-relation: the deeper into the dream the boy went, the greater grew the persistence to finding the answer to the dream. The greater that effort, the worse the headaches grew.

The doctor at this point felt that they were, for the first time in a long time, on the right path. The doctor asked the boy to slowly redevelop the dream he seemed to be having prior to the headaches.

"I can see a faint image of a person at the end of a long dark tunnel, and as I yell out for help they seem to look past me.

The louder I yell out for help, the more oblivious they seem to my need; it is as if I am yelling but no words are coming out as far as their ears can deduce.

The more I struggle to get up and help myself, the more, for some reason, I can't even stand up.

The worse the situation grows, the greater the pain. The greater the pain, the more exhausted I am. As I awake from the dream sequence, I have an excruciating headache!"

With this powerful and confusing story drawn out from the dream, the boy became more curious about the dream.

The doctor had the boy keep a journal of everything done each day, eaten each day and thought about each day. The boy was specifically to trace as much information with as great a detail as possible every time he had a headache sequence. It took only two bad headache sequences for the doctor to recognize that the dreams were somehow connected to the pain the boy had endured for more than a year now. These were the very headaches that had left doctors on the verge of conducting exploratory brain surgery in pursuit of a demon tumor that they felt was eluding their best technology and their best experts.

What the boy had realized was that the dreams scarred him so much and his energies perpetuated the dreams as he poured all of his energies into trying to determine what the dream meant . . . the long dark hallway . . . the light at the end of the tunnel or hallway . . . the figure of a person at the end of that tunnel or hallway. Why he could not just stand up; Why, as he yelled, no words seemed to come out. All of these were questions that he sought answers to.

The psychiatrist offered another idea and that was instead of focusing so much energy on trying to find the solution or answer to what the dream meant, let's back up and ask some questions about the dream itself, to see what may be revealed.

With an understanding that after each dream would ensue these painful headache sequences, the doctor met with the parents to share the revelation.

Before the doctor even completed the dream story, the parents looked at each other and immediately knew exactly what the dream related to!

The parents shared a story of when the boy was but a toddler. He had somehow come upon an open door in the home they had lived at the time. The door opened to a set of wooden stairs that emptied down upon a cement basement floor. The boy had fallen down the stairs, unknown to the parents and older children who were rushing through the house looking for the missing baby toddler. Several of them had looked down those same stairs, but with the foot of the stairs being unlighted, no one immediately saw the little boy at the base.

As a teenage boy looking backward upon that dream, he recognized that one is capable of communicating in sentences and standing upright. He was examining the event from the vantage point of a young adult and not in terms of a baby. From a baby's perspective, a baby obviously can't talk or stand and that was the disconnect in the boy's head to the frightening dreams woven nightly.

The doctor recognized that that which pained the boy was not the 'answer' but the 'question' that needed to be asked.

What was even more astonishing is that when the boy, the parents and doctor all met and the shadows of the dream were illuminated, the boy never had the dreams again. The dreams that were connected to such painful headaches immediately ceased as well!

What the parents revealed is that when the boy was just a toddler he had fallen down the stairs, and due to his age he could not speak nor walk. Once the youth had heard that, it was as if the shadows to the dreams were now clear.

What became evident to me as that boy living this experience is that when you focus energies on looking for the answer, as we are all conditioned to do, it will take you significantly longer to get to an answer, and you will endure needless pain. If you change your approach and start by asking the hard, penetrating questions, the answers will always reveal themselves to you as blatantly obvious!

The dream and the message of the dream were awaiting the appropriate question that would clarify the message of the dream. Putting the message of the dream into perspective makes the message clear and then the answer understandable. Finding the appropriate question that makes the message possible is the objective.

That, too, is the formula for success in both personal and professional relationships and situations.

Seek first to ask the hard, penetrating questions and the answers will always reveal themselves. Seek first the answer and frustrations and painful stress may more likely be your bedfellow.

The answer IS the end destination and directing mental energies at the end point causes one to inevitably miss the present questions necessary to effectively analyze subjects.

Look for tools, techniques, training and models that will aid you in asking relevant questions wherever you are and open your mind to the answers that reveal themselves to you!

Dreams are not just stories, as most would have you believe. One has to find an appropriate 'question', for them to be an 'answer'—what questions lie within the shadows of your dreams?

The Dream Was Not The Answer, It Was The Question!

The Shadows In Your Mind Are The Dreams One Weaves . . . .

Turning Mistakes Into Opportunity

by Bob Oros

Turning Mistakes Into Opportunity

by Bob Oros

Our attitude toward mistakes can either strengthen or destroy us. If we regard each mistake as a serious setback in our path to achievement, that is exactly what it will become. If we choose to regard mistakes as building blocks instead of stumbling blocks, they will then strengthen us. The secret is to look at failures as opportunities to learn.

Because we need the approval and acceptance of ourselves and of others, mistakes are embarrassing. If important people in our early environment—parents, teachers, or a boss in an early job—emphasized perfection and over reacted to our mistakes, we may have regarded this as evidence of our own lack of talent or self-worth. As a consequence, we may find we are still freezing up when a decision is needed for fear of making a mistake.

We may have avoided the entire learning process and adopted a mode of behavior that involves following only the safe path in life. The fear of failure breeds timidity and makes us hesitate to accept a challenge. The result of such a negative response to mistakes is that we fail to try something new, leaving our potential talents and abilities lying unused.

No one enjoys making mistakes. But, on the other hand, mistakes mark progress. We can choose to accept a mistake as a failure or as a lesson in progress. Our attitude toward mistakes and failures gradually conditions us either to success or to mediocrity.

The truth is that there is more to be gained by making mistakes than by avoiding them. Those who have too great a fear of making mistakes take no risks and, obviously, won't make any mistakes. But neither will they learn and grow.

Financial institutions build their public images and reputations on stability, security, safety and reliability. But if loan officers take no risks or take too few risks in making loans, the institution will not grow. Loan officers, who never make a bad loan, may be reprimanded by their superiors for losing out on additional business that might carry a risk. In short, the individual who plays it too safe is actually in greater jeopardy than more venturesome colleagues.

To develop a healthy attitude toward mistakes and failures, choose to see them as opportunities. See them as opportunities that are uniquely your own. They belong to you, and no one else can reverse them or benefit from them. Conditions become serious problems only if we choose to see them in that light. Without mistakes, there is no progress. We can learn from each mistake.

"I have learned that success is to be measured not so much by the position that one has reached, as by the obstacles which are overcome while trying to succeed," wrote Booker T. Washington.

We are destined for success. The conditions that threaten to divert us from our goals of success are artificial. They melt away and disappear whenever we expand our self-image, shore up our confidence and use mistakes as mere building blocks for constructing our own success.

All of us make mistakes. All of us wish we made fewer mistakes. And it seems as though we all vow never to make the same mistake twice. However, here is a little-known fact—the more time we spend studying our mistakes, the more likely we are to increase the number of mistakes we make.

What if we took a completely different approach and duplicated the scientific approach used by the successful corporations. For instance, corporations study the relative profitability of their products. Profits permit companies to grow, in much the same way our successes challenge you and me to grow. The companies that grow the most have focused and improved on what they have done successfully. Did they do it by concentrating on their least profitable products or services? Do they constantly review their mistakes over and over again? No. They increase their profits by concentrating on the products and services producing the most profit.

What does this mean to our success? It means that our

opportunities can be limitless, if we concentrate on our successes rather than our mistakes. That doesn't mean we stop making mistakes. It means we change our attitude toward mistakes. Instead of saying "If only I had done it this way or made a better decision," we view the mistake for what it is, something that doesn't work. We replace the "If only" with "Next time" and move on.

Let's look at it from another perspective. Suppose you know two different people. One seems to fail at whatever they attempt. The other is very successful and does exceptionally well in one specific area. Whose experience should you study to benefit most: the repeated failure, or the success? Whose secret would you rather know?

Every successful person likes to be in the company of other successful people. This companionship seems to establish a "climate" in which success grows.

Consequently, since we want to be more successful, we want to study the experiences of successful people, rather than those of the failure. Successful people make plenty of mistakes; however they relive their achievements and successes rather than their mistakes and failures.

We will never be free of mistakes nor can we become successful by simply trying to avoid mistakes. We have many successes and we have many failures. However, if corporations can increase their profits by identifying their greatest "pay-off" products and services, we may be able to do it too.

Thomas Edison's biographies show him to be a person who was not concerned with mistakes and failures. He did not spend his time trying to avoid repeating his mistakes. Edison's main concern was always with achieving his objectives. We must be concerned with what we want rather than trying to avoid what we don't want.

The answer is to become well acquainted with our successes. This doesn't mean we are going to dwell on past achievements—it means we are going to build on them rather than build on our mistakes. We begin by looking into our pasts to become better acquainted with that unique, successful person that we know we are. What we are looking for are achievements, successes and accomplishments. Remember, successful companies spend millions of dollars a year in advertising to proclaim the merits of their products and services.

What if we feel uneasy about some of the wrong decisions we have made? The traditional "rules for success" would have us set a goal and work hard until we get there. Many determined people have reached success that way, but just as often the results can be tragic. In today's changing economy the distant goal selected at the age of twenty can turn out to be a dead end at forty. And then tradition would have you believe it is too late to start over. It's never too late to find the gold nuggets buried deep within. However, like gold, they must be "panned." We should not let our past dictate our future.

You and I were born with a gift, a unique "service" we can provide. Something we can do better than anything else we do, something that comes easy and seems natural. This special talent may be apparent at an early age, or it may not surface until much later in life. All successful people the world over have found the opportunities for their own special talents and acted upon those ways to achieve their goals. Why wait for the time to pass? There's never a better time than now.

"Anyone who stops learning is old, whether at twenty or eighty," said Henry Ford. "Anyone who keeps learning stays young. The greatest thing in life is to keep your mind young."

We each hold the key to our own success, and it can only be found in our individual achievements. We must begin our search by looking in our past and thinking about our successes, not our mistakes. These nuggets are like the successful products and services the corporations concentrate on to produce the most profit.

What have I done right? What right choices have I made? What do I really enjoy doing that benefits others and gives me a feeling of satisfaction? What about money?

Did you ever make financial mistakes? Did your parents ever complain about money? Did they say people must work hard to earn a living? Did they indicate they thought money was hard to come by? Did their actions convey the feeling that money is a serious matter? All these messages are picked up by the child and serve to condition the young person. These messages get through and leave their cruel mark on the child's mind.

Once we become conditioned, our experience in the real world validates our belief that acquiring money is difficult. Jobs become hard to find and keep. Bill-paying becomes a struggle. We barely make ends meet. We find money impossible to save. Money worries eventually consume us, and we go deep into debt.

We can unlearn what we have learned. Most of the negative conditioning can be overcome. The same methods that produce negative attitudes can reverse the trend and allow the individual to develop new, positive attitudes. What we have created, we can either reverse or recreate. If our personality was shaped by daily exposure to fear, doubt and worry, we can remold it by daily exposure to more positive influences that we consciously choose. In this way, we can shape our own destiny; we can be the architects of the life we choose to live. If we are brainwashed to believe that we have no potential, it is because we have allowed it to be so. We have chosen to accept that false information. But you were created for greater and more worthwhile aspirations.

Don't waste time visiting your mistakes or losses. Look for a positive lesson to learn in times of failure or defeat. Don't look for excuses, justifications, or rationales. Grow from your mistakes.

The House

Linda, I wish you the best of
everything and always remember to
take care of yourself.

Respectfully,

by Carl Potter

The House

In the business of professional speaking and consulting, I have had the privilege of meeting many people. I have always been the type of person to help people to be more than they are. Some of these people have been THRIVERS while others are just survivors. THRIVERS are people who are doing something to improve themselves or their situations. People who spend their time waiting for something to happen are survivors. I like to work with and help a THRIVER not a survivor. This is because it takes a lot of energy to get a survivor to move. A THRIVER already has a mindset to do something and is likely headed in the right direction; they're just looking for a boost. Helping a THRIVER is also like money in the bank—it's a good investment for the future. What is my definition of a THRIVER? Simply put, an individual envisioning himself or herself greater than he or she is, committed, stable in growth, and striving for constant improvement. A short time ago, I was blessed with the opportunity to help a THRIVER. It was a wonderful opportunity to help with, "the house."

Sharon comes to my office to clean and pick things up on a regular basis. Sharon is a hard worker, someone who holds down a regular job while doing other odd jobs. She does these odd jobs to help make life more comfortable for her and her three sons. Like many women and men, Sharon is a single parent. She is pleasant and there is a sense of what some people call Kharma that is all around her as she works. When Sharon is working, she shows the diligence of a dedicated servant. But on this day something was different; something was on her mind.

Sharon came into my office and asked if I would give her some advice. Well, one thing you can get from a consultant and professional speaker is advice, even when you don't ask for it. I had just made a business phone call and was on hold waiting for an account representative when she came in. So I said, "Sure, have a seat."

Sharon began by reminding me that she was a single mom with three growing boys. "We live in an apartment, and it is small and not a great place to raise three robust boys. My full-time job is at the school across town and it was very unhandy. I need a house, with a yard that my boys can run and play in. Nothing fancy, just a house that we can turn into a home," she said. Her passion was evident and this was not just a passing thought. She was serious.

Sharon said that the big obstacle to her getting a house was saving money for the down payment and closing costs. Sharon also said that she had been praying every day that God would meet the need. "I'm sorry for taking up your time," she said, "and I realize that you are very busy, but I kept getting this feeling that I should speak to you about this." She seemed a little embarrassed and continued, "I can't explain it, I just feel impressed to talk to you about 'the house'."

Then I said, "I know why," and I reached over and turned the phone off to disconnect the call I was trying to make.

So, I began to tell Sharon why I knew she was supposed to ask me. I began to tell Sharon that a few days ago I received a call from another lady that needed some advice. "I've known this lady for many years. She recently was laid off from her job and is having some financial difficulty. She needs to sell her house and I was buying it for an investment. The call I was making was to the mortgage company. You see, her house is a burden to her, and she just needs to get out from under the mortgage to save her credit rating. She is looking for someone to pay her a small sum of money and assume the payment so that she can move. The loan is assumable and the closing cost is only $550. I was going to buy the house as an investment, but I think it is meant for you."

Sharon looked at me in shock and said, "I can't believe it!" She began to ask me about the house. Well, instead of telling her, I just called the lady with "the house" and explained to her what was going on. The lady was very happy to hear the news. They made plans to get together that afternoon so Sharon could see the house and start the buying process. When Sharon left, I asked her to keep me updated.

That evening Sharon called to tell me the house was perfect. "It is exactly what I wanted. The mortgage company is going to work with me and they feel I will have no trouble qualifying." The lady with "the house" was also very pleased. This was a win-win situation; however, the lady with "the house" had decided to become a survivor, while Sharon was continuing to be a THRIVER.

Many people will say, "Oh, things like that just happen." But this is just one of the examples I could tell you about how a THRIVER works. Sharon was a diligent THRIVER in her prayers and was working as if the prayer had been answered. I believe we all have several paths to choose from. It is our choice which path we take and choosing the correct path is sometimes a matter of paying attention and having faith that it will happen. Stumbling often puts us on a path that takes us past many people whom we could help. THRIVERS are constantly seeking opportunities to help others.

Every second of every day we should be seeking opportunities to help others. As a self-proclaimed THRIVER, I do every day what I love to do—helping others succeed in business and life. I believe that we should thrive and not just survive. That is why I teach people to become THRIVERS and not just survivors. My daily prayer is that my borders be widened. I know that widened borders will present opportunity to help someone and strengthen my relationships. Because of my relationships, God, my family, business partners and friends, everyday I move a little farther and a little higher! THRIVERS create opportunities.

What are you expecting? Do you expect to win the lottery? Get that new boat, car or other material possession? Or will you become a THRIVER so that you can be more effective in others' lives like some people in recent history?

Gandhi never had wealth, as we perceive it. Mother Teresa didn't have wealth many wish to have. What they did seemed to be pure sacrifice for others. However, for them it was a higher calling and not a sacrifice. They are remembered today for what they did for others and not for the amount of wealth they had.

Andrew Carnegie was one of the richest men in the world. In life and in death he gave his money away to help others. He also was a builder of character, demanding much from his partners and business associates and even more from himself. Andrew Carnegie was wise and wealthy. When seeking the wealth of the world, we should seek wisdom first.

Some have won lotteries, becoming instant millionaires. Without wisdom a few years later they will owe more than they won. Some have had fame and power handed to them only to find they were still lonely and sad. Wisdom is widening your borders so you can make an impact on others. Much like Ray and Barbara Wragg of British Columbia.

When this couple won 10.8 million dollars in the British Lottery, they had the wisdom to help others. First, they helped their immediate family; then they improved their own lifestyle, investing several million for cash flow purposes, and then they began seeking people who needed a boost. For instance, Sheffield Children's Hospital was one of the recipients of their gift. A $14,000 gift was given to provide a trip to Walt Disney for critically-ill kids. They also are reinvesting $14 a session in the lottery so that they can help more people just like they did in the beginning. Ray and Barbara Wraggs are THRIVERS just like Sharon who is helping herself and her boys at the same time.

Sharon wants the best opportunities for her boys. There is no doubt when a house becomes a home its borders will widen. When a mom like Sharon prays and works for what she knows will make boys into men, she is a THRIVER! Being a THRIVER gave us both a reward we will long remember.

I was given the blessing of being involved in "the house." It was a tough decision because I had been looking for rental property. "The house" would have rented for more than the payment. That's called financial wealth. The real wealth for me is knowing that Sharon is going to have a chance to raise her boys in "the house" and make it "a home."

Defining Your Own Success

by Kent Rader

Defining Your Own Success

by Kent Rader

Many business people I meet dislike their career or, at best, their present job. Research has found half of the people working today dislike their job and two-thirds of those disliked them enough that they were looking to change careers. What a sad statistic that our country has such unhappiness in its workforce.

The American business landscape and our consumer-driven society have enslaved too many people to jobs and careers which they dislike and even detest. Television commercials are even playing to this unhappiness.

Have you seen the commercial comparing the two executives, one who had a wise investment plan and the other who didn't? The one that had the wise investment plan is wearing shorts, running shoes and a T-shirt. He is doing the things that people believe they will do in their retirement. He is seen shopping at an open air market, watching the sun set on a pier, and driving a convertible on a secluded, country road. The executive that didn't have his wise investment plan continues to slave at his job. You see him commuting to a downtown office building, working late in his office, eating Chinese take-out food amidst the darkness of night over the city.

Yes, the message is clear. Invest your money wisely with our company and you can leave that job you hate. You can begin doing the things in your life you have always wanted to do. If you don't, be prepared to stay enslaved to the grind of daily work.

During a trip last summer, I was confronted with this situation by my own brother, Michael. I had a speaking engagement in Madison, Wisconsin, and things had gone beautifully. My career as a professional speaker was really taking off, and I found myself excited about the future. I took the opportunity to spend the evening with Michael and his family in Chicago before flying home. The following morning we went to a fast food restaurant for breakfast when Michael said to me, "In nine and-a-half years, I can retire." His matter of fact tone and the sadness in his voice broke my heart.

My flight to Oklahoma City, as well as my two-and-a-half hour drive to my home in rural Oklahoma, were haunted with the words of my brother. "Nine-and-a-half years and I can retire." It sounded to me like a man serving a prison term. "Nine-and-a-half years and I will be free of these shackles. Nine-and-a-half years of fighting the Chicago traffic. Nine-and-a-half years of dealing with incompetent supervisors. Nine-and-a-half years of fighting the unions. Nine-and-a-half years and I can do the things I want!" It makes me sad just writing these words today! It seems like a poor trade-off to me. Nine-and-a-half years of doing something I dislike so that I can spend my final years doing what I want. What if I don't have that long following that period of enslavement?

Michael has options, but, as he told me while writing this, there are factors such as his pension, his liberal vacation time, and being home every night with his wife and 12-year-old daughter, which make it compelling enough for him to stay. I respect that, but what I hope to do here is help those who know they are in the wrong situation and want to begin defining their own success. I hope this helps those who want to stop living someone or something else's definition of what makes a life successful without worrying about what others will think or say about it.

Let's look at some of our society's definitions of success.

Today, more often than not, we equate success with earning power, salary or prodigious wealth. If a person draws a six-figure salary or accumulates millions of dollars, he must be successful, regardless of what he feels every morning when he rises from his slumber. Even if this man hates heading to the office on a daily basis, there will be those who hold him on a pedestal because of his salary. People with vast sums of money are also held in high admiration regardless of how those sums were accumulated. There are those who hold a Michael Milken in higher regard than their local educator who has helped hundreds of children improve their lives through education for the simple reason of the size of their bank accounts.

I read a few years ago that Mother Teresa and Princess

Diana died during the same week. Though both helped people who were less fortunate, it was the young, beautiful and wealthy one who captured most of the attention over the poor and saintly one. People equate money and earnings with success.

Titles also seem to be equated with success. If a person is a "CEO" or "CFO" of a large corporation, he must be successful for the simple accomplishment of reaching such a position. Few take into consideration the workers this person may have hurt along the way to get to that position. Their basic character is not examined either. Are they honest and trustworthy? Who cares? They simply look at the person's position and determine they must be successful.

I read a wonderful parody, or at least I hoped it was written as a parody, for American executives titled *What Would Machiavelli Do?* by Stanley Bing. Mr. Bing, an executive with CBS television, states the following:

"How did the rich and powerful individuals who move the earth get where they are today? Are they smarter? Faster? Better-looking? Certainly not. Some are even short and ugly. What, then, is their edge?

"The answer is simple: they're meaner. That's all."

Stanley Bing offers today's executive advice from the teachings of the Florence bureaucrat, Niccolo Machiavelli. The basic premise of these teachings is that Machiavelli would have you "do whatever is necessary" to advance your personal power, wealth and position. It is a funny book with chapters titled "He would fire his own mother, if necessary," "He would make a virtue out of his obnoxiousness," and, my personal favorite, "He would lie when it was necessary." You get the point. Many people running large corporations are not of particularly fine character and don't deserve our admiration.

There are people who understand if they can have the appearance of wealth, people will believe them to be successful. When people achieve material possessions, we assume they are successful regardless of the means in which they achieved them. This may be one of the most corrupt circumstances in our society today because it can lead individuals and families to financial ruin.

There are two factors in our society which allow this depravity to take place. The first factor is the easy availability of credit in our society today. I am amazed at the people who want to loan Twyla and me money! Daily we receive at least one offer from a credit card company to give us a new card with a credit limit almost to the level of what a teacher in Oklahoma makes for an entire year or blank checks to use at our discretion! I have seen our financial statement and know how indiscrete I can be. Neither of these appears to be a wise decision on somebody's part!

The second factor is our economy is driven by consumers purchasing products and services. Many of the goods aren't just necessities, but indulgences. In fact, about two years ago I heard a Radio Shack commercial which summed this point up perfectly.

In this commercial, the first person commented on the second person buying a new car. He asked the second person if he was the "tennis ball on a string" type of person. This was in reference to someone putting a tennis ball on a string and suspending it from the ceiling of their garage so they would know they had pulled their car in far enough. The second person stated that this new car was far too fine a piece of machinery to entrust it to a simple tennis ball on a string. He stated he had purchased from his local Radio Shack an electronic gadget which would beep when his car was far enough in the garage. The commercial ended with the quote, "Just one of the many devices you didn't know you needed at Radio Shack!"

It got me thinking. If you didn't know you needed the gadget, maybe you also didn't know you needed a fancy car? If you didn't know you needed the car and the gadget, maybe you also didn't know you needed a garage to put both in? Really, if you didn't know you needed it, do you really need it? Where does all of this fit in Maslow and Skinner's hierarchy of needs?

You will recall from your psychology classes that Abraham Maslow and B.F. Skinner stated there are five levels of needs that all people desire. They further state a person cannot move to a more advanced level until he has satisfied the needs of the current level.

The first and most basic level of needs are physiological needs. These include the need for food, water, air and clothing.

The second level is security, the need to feel safe and free of danger. The third level is social needs. This is the need to feel loved and valued. The fourth level includes ego needs, which is the need for self-esteem and recognition. Finally there is self-actualization. This fifth level is the need to reach your full potential.

In examining the appearances of success, including high-priced cars, houses, and clothing, where do these fall in the hierarchy of needs? They do not mee t your basic physical needs or your need to feel secure. I doubt they can make you feel loved, though the diamond industry will beg to differ with me on this point. They may offer you social recognition, but it isn't always based on reality as many individuals have purchased these goods on credit, not on earned money. Finally, consumer goods cannot help one reach their full potential. This is an internal process, not one to be fulfilled through products or services.

This may be the most definitive reason so many people remain in jobs and careers they dislike—because they have been entrapped into purchasing consumer goods with their credit cards. With high credit card debt, they are enslaved to the pay check of these jobs just to keep their head above water. How can one even think about moving to a career they love if they can't afford to take a cut in pay in order to start a new business or earn less because the now career doesn't pay as much as their current one?

All of these definitions revolve around the fact that our society places the title of "successful person" around someone with money or the facade of money. I read a book by Gerry Spence a few years ago that really sparked the revolution within myself to change from a career that wasn't fulfilling to one I love! In the book *Give Me Liberty*, Gerry Spence wrote:

"The new paradigm for success in America must be 'person-based' not money-based. A successful person is one who has acquired not great wealth, but great personhood. A wealthy man who has not become a person is only an empty machine powered by churning greed. The individual who has achieved personhood is a lily in perpetual bloom. The paradigm of wealth as virtue, as money as success, as profit as the ultimate human goal is the most enslaving value of all."

Last month I read a biography of Benjamin Franklin written

in 1956 by Nelson Beecher Keyes. Talk about a man who achieved great personhood! He was a leading experimenter in electrical research, trying to determine the nature of electricity and its relationship to light. In an effort to help reduce the number of house fires in Philadelphia, the largest city in the colonies at that time, Dr. Franklin developed the lightening rod. He developed the Franklin Stove, something he called the Pennsylvania Stove, in an effort to improve the efficiency of wood-burning fireplaces. In fact, with regard to the stove, the governor of the colony offered Franklin a patent for his invention, but he staunchly refused. He stated that people should welcome "an opportunity to serve others by any invention of ours and thus we should do freely and generously." How many people in our country today would take such an unselfish stand? Not many, would be my guess. All of these accomplishments were done in addition to his taking great personal and political risk to become one of the founding fathers of the American democracy.

As we turn our attention to defining *your* own success, remember to do so with deliberation on achieving great personhood instead of just wealth.

What is Your Passion?

When I got the idea to switch careers from being an accountant to being a professional speaker and author, I read a book titled *Callings: Finding and Following an Authentic Life* by Gregg Levoy. It was a book which I devoured because it came at the perfect time for me.

I want to retrace my journey in hope that it will possibly help others in defining their own success.

In the book *Callings*, Gregg Levoy talks about passion in life:

"Passion is what we are most deeply curious about, most hungry for, will most hate to lose in life. It is whatever we pursue merely for its own sake, what we study when there is no test to take, what we create though no one may ever see it. It makes us forget that the sun rose and set, that we have bodily functions and personal relations that could use tending. It is what we'd do if we weren't worried about the consequences, about money, about making anybody happy but ourselves. It is whatever we'd be tempted to sell our souls for in order to have a hundred extra years just to devote to it, whatever fills us with the feeling poet Anne Sexton was referring to when she said that 'when I'm writing, I know I'm doing the thing I was born to do.'"

I discovered a passion for speaking when I was just fifteen years old. I was a member of my local Fellowship of Christian Athletes and we had Christmas services on the mornings of our final week of school before the holidays. On Tuesday of that week, I was asked to deliver the sermon and I remember it as if it were just last week. I developed a ten-minute program around a Bible verse and recounted a story about my Grandmother Rowan and my brother Michael getting water from the well. When I delivered the punch line of this story, the crowd erupted in laughter. I ended with a bit of insight into myself, telling people something very deep and personal. When I was leaving the program for school, Jeanine James, a senior and one of the most attractive girls in the school, told me, with tears running down her cheeks, how much it meant to her. She said I had touched her deeply and then gave me a big hug.

As I left the encounter I thought, "Say, I'm onto something here. All I have to do to be good at this is to make people laugh and cry. How hard can this be?" I had made people laugh for years, being one of Richmond's class clowns. It seemed all it took to make people cry was the willingness to tell people very personal things about myself. As was told to Melvin Udall in the movie As Good As It Gets, his willingness to humiliate himself is one of his finest traits.

I took the requisite speech classes in high school and college. Even though I enjoyed these immensely, I never thought about earning a living from it. I had a definition of success that said I needed to become a professional, and the only way speech would be incorporated in my future was for me to become an attorney and practice trial law.

During the two years that led to my final decision to change careers, I was asked to deliver financial programs for various health care associations and organizations. I was very conscious to give these audiences good content but found they would enjoy them more if they laughed. I learned how to write funny stories and practiced delivering them.

I loved the feeling of helping people learn things that would improve their lives and making them laugh while learning it. When people laugh, they are transported, if only briefly, from their current cares and worries to a happier plain. I soon found that my happiest days were those in which I was "performing" in front of an audience. This passion made it even more difficult to return to the grind that was my career in public accounting. The more I was able to speak, the less I could tolerate my chosen path. I continued until the Universe spoke and forced a career change upon me.

If you didn't have to worry about money, what others would think about you, or even your personal responsibilities, what would you do? Is there a job you would rather be doing, but fear those close to you would view as beneath your abilities? Is there an activity that you are passionate about in the terms spoken by Gregg Levoy? What do you engage in that, as Anne Sexton said, you find yourself knowing you were born to do?

As you contemplate these questions, you must give yourself time and space in order to define what path would make your life a success, not in terms defined by society, but in terms of living your life to the fullest. I read somewhere during this gestation period for my new career that few people on their death beds wished they had spent more time at the office. It got me to thinking, how would I want people to remember me—by being a good accountant? No. I wanted them to remember me by being a quality professional speaker who helped people develop happier and healthier lives. As you take the time to consider your passion, think about your obituary. What do you want it to recount? What is your individual definition of success?

As you develop your passion, listen to what the cosmos is trying to tell you. Gregg Levoy says you can find hints of the right direction for your life by listening to your dreams, the aches, pains and pleasures of your body, and the events which take place in your life. The last one helped me change my own direction.

Sam Keen, in his book *Hymns to an Unknown God*, says we should, "Enter each day with the expectation that the happenings of the day may contain a clandestine message addressed to us personally. Expect omens, epiphanies, casual blessings, and teachers who unknowingly speak to your condition." At the time my discontent with accounting as a career reached its zenith, the federal government changed the reimbursement mechanism for paying home health agencies for care of Medicare patients. This was the clientéle I worked with exclusively, and I knew the majority of our clients wouldn't be able to survive this traumatic turn of fortune. I also knew I would either have to return to auditing hospitals—a task I find second only to being the custodian of a slaughter house with regard to distastefulness—find a new job or a new career.

One day the managing partner of "The Firm," as he liked to call it, asked me to meet him in his office. We discussed the future of home health and our role in that future. With the dismal future of the industry, he told me what I already had deduced. I would probably not be able to continue in that segment of the health care industry. He did say there might be an alternative which would not force me back into hospital auditing.

The managing partner told me that some of the partners of the accounting firm wanted to develop some hospital financial software. He said these partners had joined with the owners of a software company in Tulsa to form a third company for this venture. They wanted me to write the software for them as I had twelve years of hospital financial experience and was by far the most qualified person to do so. He told me about the salary, the benefits, bonus opportunities and other perks that would accompany this labor. The long-term plans for this venture was to sell the rights to the software to a large computer company and reap the financial gain so many others were seeing in the late 1990s.

Since I was tired of working for others and understood that without my expertise, this venture would not go anywhere, I said I would consider it only if I was an owner of the company. I told him I would work on it on my own time, not asking for any salary, just like the other owners. Even though I was going to be devoting more time than the others to the project, all I was asking for was an equal ownership in the business. That way, if it took off, I would also reap the reward of selling it. The managing partner, someone with whom I had long had a turbulent relationship, said he thought that was great!

Immediately I went to work on the project while performing my responsibilities to the clients of the accounting firm. About a month into this, ownership documents had still not been drafted. I mentioned it to the managing partner a couple of times because I believed these should be developed before we got too far into the program. He assured me they were being worked on, and I had nothing to worry about.

Finally, one Friday morning in my hotel room in Sulphur, Oklahoma, I received a call saying the ownership papers had been developed. The owners were having a meeting that afternoon in Tulsa to sign them, and I was requested to be there. I traveled to Tulsa for the late afternoon meeting.

During the meeting, everyone, except me, received a copy of the bylaws of the organizations. When this happened, I didn't think too much about it. When the non-disclosure statements were passed out, I, again, didn't have one to sign. I pointed out to the attorney running the meeting that I had not received one. At that moment, the managing partner spoke up and said in front of the group, "Oh, you aren't going to be an owner at the beginning of the company. You will need to work your way into that position!" Not only was I taken back by this turn of events, I could see there were other owners in the room that believed I would be an owner from the beginning.

With a look of surprise on my face, I asked, "How am expected to earn my way into an ownership position?" The managing partner said that would be worked out later. I said I felt it was important to have that worked out at the present time before I committed any more time to the project. He told me to develop a plan of how I would become an owner by the following Wednesday and he would meet with me at that time.

As I often tell my audiences, though my programs include components about developing compassion and empathy for others, I am one of the most competitive people you will ever meet. When confronted with a perceived threat, I am more inclined to follow the words of the great Lynyrd Skynyrd song, Bring It On than to retreat. This was exactly what I did on this occassion.

I spent the weekend devising a plan that I knew everyone involved would find distasteful. If they found my plan distasteful, they would be forced to make me an owner from the beginning per the original agreement. I cared nothing about preserving the software project; I was simply blinded with beating the managing partner at the game of his creation. Since I was devoting more time than anyone else to the project, they would not only have to infuse the company with capital to pay me a salary, but they would also make me the majority owner when I was allowed into ownership. If I was not made anowner in one year, they would pay me an additional lump sum payment at that time.

On Wednesday morning, I presented my plan and I knew instantly that it had the desired effect as the managing partner's neck began to turn red. This redness moved up his neck and, about the time it engulfed his entire face, he responded to my proposal by saying something that was a reflection on my ancestry. Knowing things were going my way, I stood up and countered with something he could physically do to himself. (I have since had it pointed out this is anatomically impossible, but it sounded good at the time.) At this point, one of the other partners of the accounting firm physically came between the two of us and, as we stood there staring at each other, the managing partner said I could be an owner from the very beginning. I knew I had won the game, but I didn't feel good about the situation.

This event not only cautioned me that the software situation would be one which would be fraught with distrust, but it forced me to pause to evaluate if this was something I really wanted to do. It just so happened that the Monday between these two meetings, I had presented a financial program in Wichita, Kansas. The crowd had loved it! In my hotel room that Wednesday night, I realized that my calling was to speak, not write software, do accounting or be involved with a person I found as repulsive as this managing partner!

Had I not listened to the events of my life at that moment, had I proceeded with the situation which I knew deep down in my heart was not for me, even though it offered the opportunity for tremendous financial gain, I would have possibly missed the opportunity to do what I love! Luckily I listened, but I often wonder how many times in the past the universe had tried to tell me about something and I didn't listen? The important thing was I listened that night!

What events are talking to you today? Is your career reaching a crossroad or even a dead end? Have you just reached a point in your life where you can simplify your material possessions? Has your family situation recently changed through divorce, death or kids graduating and leaving home? Listen to these events and see what they may be trying to tell you.

How To Realistically Change Careers

Okay, you say, "Kent, I know what my passion is, but I just don't know how to get from this point in my life to a place where I can do my passion." That is one of the great stumbling blocks to all of this, but, as the old saying goes, "Where there's a will, there's a way." When my own opportunity arose, I was not only faced with the possibility of losing my job at the accounting firm, but knew I didn't want to head into the software business, so I had to figure out what to do, and quickly.

Since I didn't follow my Grandmother Rowan's advice about falling in love with a rich girl as easily as I could fall in love with a poor one, I knew I had to find a way to follow my passion and earn a living.

I had four accounting clients I believed would survive the reimbursement changes of Medicare. They had utilized me for their work, in some cases, since their first days in business. If I was able to capture their full fee for myself and not incur the overhead of having an office, I would just about equal my annual salary from "The Firm".

I approached the four clients to ask if they would utilize me if I decided to leave the accounting firm? They all said they would, so I knew my income wouldn't dramatically suffer while I began the transition of careers.

Further, I contacted a company in Kansas City that put on public seminars around the country. These included financial programs that I knew I could easily do. I sent them a tape of one of my programs, a resume of my qualifications, and auditioned for them that fall in Kansas City. I was selected to do financial seminars for them and my speaking career was off!

We devised a plan for our income that included a combination of revenue from accounting work and speaking. As you devise your plan of how to transition to your new career, take into consideration that it is fine to have more than one source of income. Too many of us, myself included, are uncomfortable with having more than one source of income because it makes it difficult to answer the question, "What do you do?"

I was often tempted to answer that I am a professional speaker, though that wasn't always my largest source of revenue.

During my first year, I earned more money than any other time in my life. About two-thirds of it came from accounting revenue and one-third came from speaking. All but $600 of the speaking revenue came from engagements from the speaking company in Kansas City. I did nearly 100 engagements around the country for them! The good news was I got an enormous experience in a short period of time. It also offered me time to learn how to generate my own engagements while I was earning money speaking. The bad news was I earned only about 10% of what I would earn if the engagements were my own.

That trend quickly changed during the second year as my income was split 50-50 from speaking and accounting, 85% of the speaking revenue came from my own engagements while the remaining 15% came from the company in Kansas City.

Now that I am into my third year, it appears that 90% of my income will come from speaking, all of it from engagements I have generated on my own, and only 10% from accounting. In fact, I stopped doing accounting work earlier this year—only two-and-a-half years after going out on my own.

"To Create One's Own World In Any of The Arts
Takes Courage"

Amen! This quote from Georgia O'Keeffe says it all. In my first year, I was in Columbus, Ohio and happened to stop by the local art museum to pick up a T-shirt for Twyla. I found a coffee mug with this quote on it. For the past two years I find myself choosing it for my coffee on the mornings I need to remember to summon courage along this path.

It does take great courage to pursue your passion. Many practical and well-meaning people will tell you how foolish you are to do this. You must keep your passion in the forefront of your thoughts. With lots of hard work, a well-thought plan of action, one which considers the pitfalls of the situation, and great breaths of courage, you will reach the point in your life where you are living your definition of success daily!

I was at my hometown of Richmond, Missouri recently for my parents' fiftieth wedding anniversary. Somehow I was connived into delivering the sermon of my childhood at the church. Though the program was only twenty minutes long, I spent weeks writing and practicing for it.

As I arose to start, I saw my parents, my wife and children, my brother and his family, not to mention all of my uncles and aunts sitting in the audience. The tension within was nearly unbearable. I did my twenty minutes and, just like that Tuesday 27 years ago, my words made people laugh and cry. As I walked to the back of the church with the minister, I was engulfed in those same feelings of passion I have had following every program I have ever delivered. There were also feelings of relief and gratitude that I didn't bomb in front of the people who had been influential during my childhood.

As I stood in the receiving line greeting members of the congregation as they exited the church, one of the elderly members asked me what I did for a living. A bit perplexed by the question, I responded that I was a professional speaker and author. She, in all seriousness and with a hint of remorse, said, "Oh, so you're unemployed?" I couldn't help but laugh and said, "Yes, ma'am. Today, I am indeed unemployed!"

I may be unemployed on all but fifty days per year, but I am following my passion and defining my own success independent of others' ideas! I am thankful for this opportunity, that I have a loving and supportive family, guidance and assistance from other speakers like Michael Johnson and Jeffrey Magee, and the abilities with which I've been blessed.

Recovery . . . Ghosts From The Past

by Billy Robbins

Recovery . . . Ghosts From The Past

by Billy Robbins

It is a sight to behold, unlike anything I have ever seen! The snow-covered mountains in the distance are amazing. The crystal-clear water of the North Platte River reflects every scene as a large mirror that lay on the ground. No matter what direction you look there is totally unspoiled beauty, surpassed only by the sound! Yes, beauty like this has a sound—the sound of the river, not a roar, but a gentle, relaxing sound as it moves with ease past the boulders and rocks carved out over the centuries; the occasional creak of saddle leather and jingle of buckles and bit. The snow crunching under the hooves of my horse, Custer, added a rhythm to the surroundings. These glorious sounds mixing with the wind that passed through the trees play a medley in the background for this scene that could only have been painted by His hand.

The light is blinding. Everything is a blur, a haze. Yet through the haze, I can see faces at a distance, looking down on me from above. Suddenly, a familiar but out-of-place sound rips through the air. Ack! Ack! Ack! The rounds are incoming. The medley is replaced with screaming and cursing. Ambush! Ambush! A smothering heat replaces the cool, crisp mountain air. Everything is covered in darkness. The fear is overwhelming, like a spirit has just covered the area with the spreading of its wings. Bodies covered with sweat, now mixed with blood, fall around me.

The jungle has come alive with flashes, pops, explosions and, above it all, the terrified yelling of boys, forced to become men. I feel a burning sensation in my right leg. It's not what you would call real pain—just enough feeling to grab your attention.

Instantly, almost robotically, my hand moves to my tingling leg. I feel the warm liquid as it pours into my palm. I bring it to my face and to my amazement come to the conclusion . . . it's blood! I hear my voice join the choir of terrified yells, "I'm hit! I'm hit!

Corpsman! Corpsman!" "He's gone!" comes a reply, "Get on that *&%*%&$#@ radio and get us some *%&$#@%@ help, NOW!"

Finally, I'm reacting instead of thinking! I hear the voice on the other end of the radio as he replies to my frantic call for help, "Roger that, alpha six. The cavalry is on the way! Hang in there, buddy, we're gonna get you out!"

Rounds are going off all around—you can hear them as they cut through the jungle plant life. Waiting is always the hardest part. It all seems so unreal. Even through all the noise, above the sound of your own M-16 as you return fire, you can hear your heart pounding in your chest.

Then you hear it! In your mind it's like the sound of Michael with his band of angels, their wings outstretched and growing louder as they get closer and closer. In reality, it's an angel of death to your enemies. It's the blades of the gunships that are going to save your tail again and make sure you're able to return to fight another day.

Again, there's that blinding light. However, this time along with the faces you can vaguely see through the haze, you hear voices calling your name. It seems they are trying to call you away from the fear, the sounds and the confusion that are surrounding you.

In the chute, you're focused, you're thinking about nothing else but the ride. Eight seconds, eight seconds! The roar of the crowd, the crackling sound of the PA system are nothing but mere background noises as you concentrate on the job ahead. Stay centered; don't let him get out in front of you!

You quickly think about the conversation with friends the night before. They ask, "Why are you doing this?" They don't have a clue. Your reply: "It takes eight of the longest seconds in the world to ride a bull. But when the buzzer finally sounds, and you've stayed on for that allotted time, there are few greater highs. You've conquered fear, fate, the unknown, and successfully met the challenge of explosion and power generated by a very mean animal that weighs up to 2,000 pounds. You looked the creature in the eye, and you won!"

You're ready; the equipment is right; the creature is right; the time is right. With a simple nod of your head all hell is unleashed. Eight seconds, eight seconds! It seems like an eternity. The adrenaline is flowing; the fear factor kicks in, and you're right where you want to be. For a few seconds! Suddenly, with one quick and unexpected spin to the left, you feel all your weight shift into the rope. Your grip gives way and you're sliding down. Then all of a sudden, with a kick of those two powerful back legs, you are airborne. It has all happened in a matter of about four seconds, but to you, it's in slow motion and is going on forever. Up you go! Higher, higher! Eventually Newton's Law will kick in, and landing is always tougher than getting on.

Again, the light is blinding, the voices are louder, calling you up, up, up! I'm not falling! I'm going higher, higher! The faces are clearer this time, the haze not so thick.

"Billy, Billy, are you alright?"

It feels like I'm struggling to come alive. But where am I? What's going on? Suddenly, my mind starts to clear. Oh my God! I remember now! I look down to see a sheet pulled up to my neck. Fighting, using every ounce of strength I have, I manage to get the covers off! Looking down again, the reality of my situation has just set in. It feels like I'm lying under the weight of the whole world, pressing down on my whole being, squeezing even the smallest fragment of life out of me. They're gone! Both of them! I knew this was going to happen going in. But in the back of my mind there was always that glimmer of hope. Nothing was really going to be any different when I woke up. My hands would still be there and my life would go on. But it was not to be.

Was there this great rush of despair? No. Did depression fill the room and try to overtake me? No. Was there a feeling of self-pity or hopelessness? No! There was such a feeling of exhilaration and joy that it would be hard to describe. I was alive and still full of life! Was I the same? No! Would I ever be the same again? No! Did it matter? Absolutely not! I still had life! Though it was different than what I had ever known life to be before, it was there. It was real! It was mine! It was the most important thing in the world at that time!

These are some of the ghosts from my past. Some pleasant, some not! This is what I remember as I came to in the recovery room after the amputation of both my hands. They are small parts of my life. Not the most important in my mind, but for some reason the ones that showed themselves in a time of great unrest. Do they mean anything significant? I believe they do. I really haven't spent a lot of time analyzing it. Until now! At the time, there was too much going on to even consider it. Because, believe me, the feelings of exhilaration and joy didn't last long.

Another reality was beginning to set in. What now? What was I going to do now? My life has just taken a dramatic change, to say the least. What happens now? I had never been around any one like this before, someone with no hands. What was available? What would I be able to do? What would I not be able to do? How would I eat, get dressed, drive, brush my teeth, and a million other questions that all seemed to come on me at once. If there ever was a time to panic, to lose control, to lose hope, this was it! This was shaping up to become one of those defining moments in a person's life. I have experienced a few of these but none quite as significant as this was turning out to be.

As I look back on it all now, the things I remember in recovery—those ghosts of my past—were reappearing only in another form. It truly was one of those defining moments. I was being reminded that I could achieve this greatest goal ever set for my life. Even though it was not a goal of my own choosing–someone else that made a careless mistake set it for me. It was nothing new. I had done it all before. In order to get back the joy and peace that I experienced on that day in the mountains, I had to get my life back. It was more traumatic both mentality and physically than anything I had experienced in Vietnam. And it was going to take as much tenacity as anything I had ever tried to stay on for eight seconds in order to achieve that goal.

But we have all experienced these defining moments. Some of them are tragic, some full of laughter and joy, and some just as matter-of-fact as they could possibly be. But in all cases, I would say these defining moments are always unexpected. How we react to them and the things we learn are some of the most important lessons in life.

In my case, as I lay in the hospital contemplating the situation, I know the decisions I made there altered the entire course of my life. It was there that I seriously started planning my success. Every one of you has everything it takes to become successful. It just has to be applied properly. There are three key ingredients to success: attitude, commitment and vision. Without these, you will never be successful at anything. These three things not only brought me through my accident, but they are also the same three things that have brought me through all my past circumstances. Attitude, commitment and vision are what have brought me the success I enjoy today.

As I came back to reality in that hospital recovery room, my hands were gone, but my attitude was still intact. It was my attitude that got me through the hard times. Facing an extended stay there, lengthy rehabilitation, all the unknowns, and financial ruin; it was my attitude of "No matter what!" that got me through. I don't believe attitude is everything, but it sure comes in handy when nothing seems to be going your way. I do know that the wrong attitude will keep you out of the game forever!

Your attitude determines so many factors in your life: how you look at things in general; how you react to the circumstances you find yourself in. It doesn't matter what the circumstances are or how big they appear to be. With the wrong attitude you will never see past the circumstance and discover the answer. As the old saying goes, "Is the glass half-empty or half-full?" Your attitude determines how you view your job, your relationships . . . even your life. Stop and think about it: how much fun is it to be around someone with a lousy attitude? Not only are they miserable creatures, but they make everyone around them miserable. And it doesn't take very long for them to accomplish that.

You must be committed! Joining the Marine Corps was a commitment. I committed to serve my country and my Corps. When I went to Vietnam my commitment grew even stronger. I was committed to make it home, and as my attitude kicked in, "No matter what!" that commitment became a reality in my life. In the hospital, my commitment grew stronger every day, because it seemed every day a new obstacle arose.

How did it work? They told me I would be in there a minimum of sixteen weeks. I made a simple yet complete commitment. If I stay in this hospital sixteen weeks I will go completely insane. I'm getting out of here as soon as possible. Attitude, "No matter what!" I was admitted into the burn center on December 8. I was released on December 31. Twenty-four days instead of one hundred and twelve.

Will it work for you? Absolutely! And it will work for you in any area of your life and business. If you are going to be successful at any endeavor you attempt in life, you have to be committed. It cannot be a half-hearted commitment either. Those will accomplish nothing in your life. Because as soon as things get hard it will crumble. A commitment has to be firm, unshakable and irrevocable! Those are the kind that will give you the stick-to-itiveness that enables you to see anything through to the end! Too many people are committed to something one day and not committed the next. Then they wonder why they never accomplish anything.

I had one vision in the hospital. It burned on the inside of me like nothing I had ever felt before. It was simple, concise, and ever in the forefront of my mind. I'm going to get my life back! I'm going to have the same kind of fun-filled, exciting, joyful life I experienced when I was on the mountaintop. Not only did I believe it, I could see it! And at that time it seemed like one impossible mountain for me to climb! Attitude: "No matter what!" Commitment: "I don't care how long it takes or what I have to overcome. It makes no difference how much it hurts or what I have to go through. What others may say or think is impossible has no bearing on what I can achieve!" Vision: "Come hell or high water, I will get my life back and it will be bigger and better than before!"

Was it a challenge? You bet! It seemed like all the so-called professionals offered me no hope. I remember when I went to rehab for the first time. It was supposed to be the best in the country. I walked in there and this lady hands me a piece of Balsa wood for one hook and a piece of sandpaper for the other. I look at this lady and ask, "What am I supposed to do with these? I came here to get my life back! I want to learn to feed myself, dress myself, go to the bathroom alone!" This poor lady looks back at me and says, "Son, I'm sorry, but you're just going to have to realize there are some things you will never be able to do again."

This lady couldn't help me! She gave me no hope! Don't you hate thinking like that? I was in therapy about forty-five minutes. They had nothing to offer me. I went home and spent the next year rehabilitating myself. There are people like this everywhere. They have terrible attitudes, won't commit to anything, and have absolutely no vision. All they can do is try to hold you back, keep you from becoming successful, and rob you of your visions and dreams. If you are hanging around with people like this, RUN NOW! Believe me, you don't need them!

These three things—attitude, commitment and vision–will work in your life, in your business, at any time. They've certainly worked for me over the years. They have not only helped me take my speaking business to the top, but they also have helped me turn a few of my failures into successes. It's just a matter of choosing what you want and how you want it. That's always the hardest part—making the choice, the decision. It has nothing to do with your color, your background or your education. It's just a matter of choices. You choose how you want to live. You choose where you want to live. You choose what you want to be. You choose what you want to do. You choose the amount of success you want to have in your life. The greatest thing about our country is we have the ability to choose. You are where you are today, not because someone or something chose for you. You're there because of every choice you have made in your life! Success is just another one of those choices.

No matter how you have lived your life, or even how long, we all carry around ghosts. Some are ever present. Some only arise out of the darkness on occasion. The presence and prevalence they take in your life is all up to you. Attitude, commitment and vision are the weapons that will conquer these ghosts. Your attitude, as always, determines your altitude. Will you allow your ghosts to hold you down, keep you from rising up and achieving your dreams? The attitude you choose to have will determine this. Your commitment will determine your success at any endeavor you attempt in life. Perhaps your greatest weapon is the vision. Your life should be one huge vision; the bigger the better. Your vision should never involve looking backward into your past. If it does, the ghosts of "I should have," "I would have," or "I could have" will forever rule the day! Always move forward, keeping your vision in front of you, because eventually, you will arrive there!!

Valuable Vision
From My Grandmother

by Jim Stovall

Valuable Vision From My Grandmother

by Jim Stovall

In this life, contrary to popular belief, we don't always get what we work for. We don't always get what we earn. We don't always get what we want. We don't even always get what we need. We do, without fail, get what we believe that we deserve.

Human beings are always seeking their comfort level. Our comfort level is generally defined by what we think we deserve or what we can mentally picture ourselves experiencing.

Every once in a great while, a person comes along who drastically elevates our vision of our own value. My grandmother was just such a person for me. I can't begin to tell you what a special person she was in my life. Shortly after I had lost my sight, my grandmother came to visit me in Tulsa.

Grandmother and I always had a very open, honest relationship, but up to the time of that visit, we had never talked about my being blind. After she had been in our home two or three days, she said, "Jim, when you get a chance, I'd like for you to come to my room. We need to talk a minute." I immediately went with her to her room, and she closed the door and said, "Now, don't say anything and don't argue with me. I've already talked to your grandfather about this. This spring, I want to see my flowers one more time, and then I want you to call your doctor on the telephone and tell him to do an operation to take out my eyes and give them to you."

My grandmother didn't know that such an operation wasn't possible for the restoration of my sight, but her saying that to me was just as valuable to me as if I had had such an operation and could see fully today.

Her offer increased my self-worth, self-esteem, and value. Even though I had lost my sight, I caught a new vision of who I could become and my belief in what I deserved went up immeasurably.

Once we have caught a new vision and begin to believe in our destiny, we can start moving toward our goal through the vehicles that present themselves to us. In my case, my vehicle took the form of business success via selling and marketing. Here, my grandmother had some lessons to teach me as well.

Rarely do we fail because we don't know what to do. We fail because we don't do what we know. Success is simple. It's not easy, but it's very uncomplicated.

Selling and marketing are the keys to multiplying our success. Whether it's in a personal relationship or a professional one, our ability to communicate ideas and convey concepts will determine how far we will go. Selling is the highest-paid profession in the world and, remember, no one makes any money until someone sells something.

For years, I have trained people on how to sell and market their products or services. I thought I was really good at it until I got the million dollar advice.

During another visit with my grandmother, she asked me to help her clean out her basement. I reminded her that of all the family members present, I was the only one who was blind. That didn't seem to matter much to her, so I followed her downstairs, and we began sorting through boxes.

I came across a box that seemed to be filled with very old greeting cards. There was a ribbon on top of the box. I remember asking my grandmother about it, and to my surprise, she told me that she used to earn money selling greeting cards. I had never known her to be anything other than a housewife, so I was very curious.

I asked what the ribbon was for, and she told me that she had been the top greeting card salesman for the entire year. This had been during the Depression when it must have been difficult to sell anything, but I had a very high opinion of my own sales training ability, so I decided to ask her some questions.

I asked, "Grandma, how do you handle objections?"

I thought this was a pretty basic question for anyone in the world of sales, but she promptly replied with her own question, "What's an objection?"

I sighed and patiently explained to her that an objection was when your potential customer is giving you an excuse for why they won't buy. I will never forget her response. She said, "Jim, if I'm standing at someone's doorstep four weeks before Christmas, and I am cold and tired, when they tell me they don't want to buy my greeting cards, I'm not going to argue with them, I'm going to go to the next house. Because I have always felt that if you're going to sell, you should sell to people who buy."

This is among the most profound business lessons I have ever learned.

Several years later, I was asked to be a keynote speaker at the Million Dollar Round Table, which is the Super Bowl for motivational speakers. It is an event held annually, and only the top salespeople worldwide in the insurance industry are invited. I was privileged to be asked to share the stage with Christopher Reeve.

I told my grandmother's advice to the 5,000 people assembled, and I left the stage to a thunderous standing ovation. As I was making my way backstage, the chairman of the organization told me he had never heard an ovation like that before. As he had missed my presentation—being busy backstage with other activities—he asked what I had shared with the top sales people in the world that could generate that kind of reaction.

I told him, "It's simple. If you're going to sell, be sure to sell to people who buy."

I know he was bewildered with the simplicity of the message, but all great truths come disguised as oversimplistic.

The only person you really have to sell on your goal is you. As long as you're convinced, no one can take it from you or discourage you. When they reject your idea, you'll merely chalk it up to timing, focus, or maybe they're just in a different place in their life.

You are the only customer that matters, so keep selling to yourself and stay sold on your destiny.

While we're on this theme of wisdom from my grandmother, now would be a good time to attack your personal mission statement.

One of the new fads in corporate America is the mission statement. Every one-man operation up to the largest multinational corporation has to have a mission statement.

While I applaud this practice as a wonderful way to establish a collective direction for an organization, it is much more critical that each individual has a personal mission statement. You have got to know why you are here and what your top priority is on a daily basis.

Once you have established a personal mission statement, then you can weigh and prioritize each activity as to its impact on helping you reach your goal. If you don't know specifically where you're going, it's impossible to determine how to get there or which activities will help you along the way.

My personal mission statement was given to me by my grandmother. She was very ill at the end of her life, and we all knew it wouldn't be long. She had expressed her wish to stay at home, as opposed to being in the hospital, so arrangements were made for hospital equipment, nurses, etc., to be available at her house.

One of the last times I went to visit her, her nurse told me that my grandmother was very proud of me and all of the things that I do. I was quite surprised by this, as I wasn't sure she ever knew exactly what I did in my career.

The nurse explained to me that my grandmother had a picture on her nightstand of me holding the Emmy award and that my grandmother told everyone who came to visit her, "This is my grandson. He does two things: he helps blind people see television, and he travels all around the world telling people they can have good things in their lives."

As I look back on it now, I realize that she understood my destiny better than I did.

You have got to reduce your life goals into what I call an "elevator speech." If you cannot explain it to a total stranger in 20 seconds, you really haven't defined it in your own mind. If it's not defined in your own mind, there is no possibility you will ever live it out in your own life.

Anyone who has ever succeeded at anything in this world has combined the elements of passion and focus. Passion gives you power and energy. Focus gives you direction and endurance. Unless your personal value is high, your conviction is strong, and your mission is clear, you have no hope of living out your dreams.

I hope that the lessons my grandmother taught me will open as many doors in your life as they have in mine. Today, I get paid a great deal of money for making speeches, writing books, and creating newspaper columns that people seem to think are filled with an incredible amount of unique wisdom. In reality, the wisdom came from a very special old lady in my life who shared complex concepts in the simplest terms. The things that people pay a great deal of money to learn, I was given as a free gift of love and came to understand these things simply as a way to live one's life.

I look forward to your success and, as I end each of my weekly columns . . . Today's the day!

ABOUT THE AUTHORS

Dr. Joani Bedore

Dr. Joani Bedore, a Feldman Award-winning college instructor from Oklahoma, gave up a lifetime teaching career to start PEACEMAKER Seminars, Inc. Her one-day Peaceful Heart Seminar offers an unforgettable, life-changing new approach to stress and anger management on the job.

For compelling business reasons, her facilitators teach people to be peaceful at work. This is because stressed out, angry workers are dangerous to the bottom line. They are also less productive.

The Peaceful Heart Seminar offers a simple solution. In a full day of reflective learning and self-renewal, workers explore nine powerful ideas that they will use for the rest of their lives.

You can also get the popular PEACEMAKER CD (with 16 uplifting songs by award-winning Minnesota songwriter Ann Reed) at our site.

To schedule seminars for your company, contact:

PEACEMAKER Seminars, Inc.
263 S. Cincinnati, #441
Tulsa, OK 74105

or visit:
www.peacemakerseminars.com

Dawn L. Billings, M.A., LPC

Dawn is the founder and president of Beyond Empowerment, Inc. and To Touch A Life, companies dedicated to creating human moments that make life worth living and inspire people to make their dreams a reality. She travels nationally speaking as an expert on leadership—greatness and children—practical, powerful parenting—creating our lives out of the future for which we dream, and violence prevention.

Dawn has a masters degree in clinical psychology and is a licensed professional counselor. She has been in private practice fifteen years working with individuals, couples, and families. She is ABD (all but dissertation) toward her Ph.D. in Organizational Psychology.

She is the author of several books *GREATNESS & CHILDREN: Learn the Rules,* and a workbook *Choose to BE GREAT* and coauthor with her twelve-year-old son Corbin of *The ABC's of Becoming Great, Possibilities I: Awakening the Leadership Potential Within, The ABC's of Great Leadership,* and *The ABC's of Peace and Compassion.* Dawn is also a contributing author to *Chicken Soup for the Christian Family Soul,* which was released in 2000.

Dawn can be reached to purchase books or to schedule a speaking engagement at (918) 200-3296 fax (918) 298-7077or e-mail — ToTouchALife@aol.com.

John Irvin, CSP

John Irvin resides in Tulsa, Oklahoma (where everything is O.K.) and is the president of Lifestyle Enhancement Services (LES), a successful motivational and consulting business.

LES offers keynotes, seminars and workshops that are designed to enhance conferences, conventions, annual meetings, trainings and special events. In fact, LES will make any meeting a special event!

John, a graduate of the University of Tulsa, has been creating "playful opportunities" for personal and professional growth for over twenty five years. Today, as the creator of *Hilarity Therapy® Programs*, and other programs of "attitude enrichment," John shares from his work in corporate training, leisure sciences, mental health and health and wellness education the message that each of us has the ability to enjoy doing more and be more than we currently are, and have great fun while doing it!

John Irvin is a member of the American Association for Therapeutic Humor, the National Speakers Association, the Oklahoma Speakers Association, the American Society for Training and Development, the Humor and Health Institute, the Association for Experiential Education, Project Adventure, Inc., and the International Jugglers Association.

John has also authored two joke books, *Chicken Poop In My Bowl*, and *Chicken Poop In Your Bowl, II*. He is also a contributing author in the anthology, *Possibilities: Awakening Your Leadership Potential.*

For more information on John Irvin and his programs, contact:

Lifestyle Enhancement Services
P. O. Box 4397
Tulsa, Oklahoma 74159-0397

888-997-PHUN
www.johnirvin.com
john@johnirvin.co

Dr. Michael Johnson

Dr. Michael Johnson is a former professional rodeo cowboy who became an industrial psychologist and university professor. He now travels nationally speaking to corporate industry and educational associations sharing his beliefs on how we can truly empower, persuade and motivate others to live richer lives.

In addition to being an author, singer and songwriter, he appears on national public radio and television as a storyteller and is a columnist for two national magazines.

The theme of all his work, found in books, stories and song, is a message of encouragement to discover the power within each of us to live more abundant lives . . . and to become aware that when we do what is in our hearts, helpers will be placed in our path to aid us on the journey. Other works include *Susie; The Whispering Horse, The Most Special Person, Cowboys and Angels, and Tad Pole and Dr. Frog.*

When at home, Michael spends his time writing. He also spends a good deal of time thinking about the successes of his rodeo days, while conveniently forgetting the failures. Using this process, he has become in his own memory a much better cowboy than he ever was in real life.

Michael lives on a horse farm in rural Oklahoma.

Dr. Michael Johnson

Texan by birth
Cowboy by the grace of God

Rt. 1 Box 234
Idabel, Oklahoma 74745

Michaelspeaks@msn.com
580-286-7784
www.brownbooks.com

Rhett Laubach

Rhett Laubach energizes and informs audiences through his 200 keynotes, seminars and conferences per year. Over the past ten years, high schools, colleges, and student organizations have comprised 90% of his clientele. Rhett's programs focus on character education and leadership skill development.

His programs are high energy, high interaction and high content. One audience member said, "Being on the receiving end of Rhett's presentation is not a spectator sport!"

Rhett's company, YourNextSpeaker.com, is a value-added component of his speaking endeavors. His clients can choose from five different speakers, including Stewart Kennedy, president of Kennedy Foods and inventor of the new sliced peanut butter product, P.B. Slices.

In 2000, Rhett assumed the role of market innovator for Kennedy Foods. His responsibilities include researching and developing opportunities within the grocery retail and food whole-sale industries.

Rhett was born and raised in the small, rural farming community of Laverne, Oklahoma. He graduated from Oklahoma State University with a bachelor's degree in agricultural economics. Rhett lives in Tulsa, Oklahoma with his wife, Ashley.

Rhett Laubach
1703 S. Quaker
Tulsa, OK 74120

405.880.3946
810.454-7556 fax
rhett@yournextspeaker.com
www.yournextspeaker.com

Jeff Magee, CSP

With more than twenty years of experience as an entre-
preneur and business owner, Jeff started his first business at age
15 and sold it to a major advertising firm before going to college!

Dr. Jeffrey Magee, PDM, CSP, CMC, is an award-winning
business journalist, was rated the number one salesman in the
nation by a Fortune 500 firm in 1988, has produced multiple audio
development programs, has written fourteen books—four
have been best sellers—and is the publisher of *PERFORMANCE®*
magazine.

As a certified Professional Direct Marketer (PDM) and
Certified Speaking Professional (CSP), and Certified Management
Consultant (CMC), he heads up JEFF MAGEE INTERNATIONAL®,
a leading residential skill development and consulting firm locat-
ed in Tulsa, OK, and is Co-Founder/Chairman-of-the-Board of
WAREHOUSE:Intellect.com—a leading e-based training develop-
ment firm based out of Minneapolis, MN with contracts with
Fortune 100 firms and the Department of Defense!

He is a speaker/trainer favorite with Fortune 500 busi-
nesses, associations and convention audiences internationally,
and each year he speaks to groups worldwide. The London Times
has called him "an American business guru."

Jeff has served as the President and Co-President of the
Oklahoma Speakers Association and has been recognized as their
"Professional Speaker & Member of the Year" two consecutive
years running.

For more self-development and
professional development resources by
Magee, go to www.JeffreyMagee.com. To
find out more about having Jeff present one
of his content-rich programs that do more
than motivate and educate—they provide
you with immediate applicable action plans
to generate lasting results—check out
www.JeffreyMagee.com/Planners.asp or
email Robert@JeffreyMagee.com or call toll
free 1-877-90-MAGEE.

Bob Oros

Bob Oros is best known for his sales training seminar and book *CUTTING EDGE SALES,* which has been presented over 1300 times to more than 25,000 salespeople.

Prior to starting his speaking career in 1992, Bob spent 25 years working his way from a street salesperson to the position of National Sales Manager for a Fortune 200 Company. During one year alone, he initiated contracts resulting in THIRTY MILLION DOLLARS IN NEW ANNUAL BUSINESS.

Bob has worked as a General Manager for a distribution center, owner of a food brokerage company, a buying group regional manager and a national sales manager.

Bob has also been a contributing editor for *Institutional Distributor Magazine* for over ten years and has sold over 25,000 copies of his book, *CUTTING EDGE SALES.*

For more information contact

Bob Oros Sales Training

405-751-9191

bob@orossalestraining.com

Carl Potter

Carl Potter is a business development and management consultant who works with organizations that want to gain more clients, build value and gain more revenue from existing clients. Carl's presentations are content rich, and full of enthusiasm. Carl is known by those he works with as an encourager and coach. With a passion to see others succeed, he encourages participants to grow through continuous personal improvement.

Carl achieves this goal by involving listeners with effective humor and real-life examples. He believes that successful people are those who learn from mistakes (his as well as others) and drive on to success. You'll find that Carl relates well, provokes thought and stimulates personnel at all levels of organizational structure. Many people who leave corporate life are told, "You need to call this guy." People, who do call Carl for coaching and mentoring, will tell you of his never-ending energy and positive attitude.

Carl is the author of *Thriving Business* a step-by-step process designed to guide anyone needing more clients in their business. He has also authored *Introduction to Supervision*, co-authored *Possibilities, In Celebration of Customer Service* and *The Accident Prevention Workbook*.

As Founder and President of Potter and Associates Inc., Carl utilizes his 30-plus years of business, corporate experience and personal network to help the clients he serves. Potter and Associates provides their clients with consulting, training resources, seminars, workshops and keynote speakers.

If you are interested in motivating your organization to thrive and not just survive or need a speaker who can motivate your employees or association members, call Potter and Associates, Inc. at 800-259-6209 or email him, carl@potterandassociates.com.

Kent A. Rader

Kent Rader is a professional speaker and author who champions the belief that developing happier, healthier employees can lead to success for any organization. Uniquely incorporated with humor, Kent's programs draw upon his management experience as C.E.O./C.F.O. of healthcare organizations, his physical training as a life-long, competitive runner, and his wife's experience as a public school art teacher. A wealth of information is offered in an entertaining environment. Healthy and happy employees contribute to success via employee retention, improved performance and creative problem-solving skills. He has presented programs throughout the United States to organizations wanting to make a positive difference in the lives of those they serve.

Kent A. Rader
American Federation of Mentors
715 North Oklahoma
Mangum, Oklahoma 73554

405-209-3273
AFMLocal200@aol.com

Billy Robbins

In December of 1980, Billy was injured in an industrial accident. The results of the accident were profound—the amputation of both his hands. Facing the overwhelming facts of his new circumstances, lengthy rehabilitation, and financial ruin, he's proven that no matter what situation you may find yourself in, your success is not only inevitable, but also fun!

Since his accident, Billy has been a successful horse breeder, businessman and entrepreneur. He is now the president of his own company, Jubilee Enterprises International, Inc., and an internationally recognized speaker and author with clients including NASA, Tropicana, Quaker Oats, Conoco, Lucent Technologies, ExxonMobil, UPS and the Departments of Defense and Energy.

He and his lovely wife, Harolronda, have five children eight-years-old and under, and yet he is still considered sane by most of his friends and colleagues. Billy thinks we have complicated life, business and success far too much and that everyone has everything it takes to be successful if just applied correctly. He believes attitude, commitment and vision, properly mixed, makes an explosive fuel that will propel you to the destination of your dreams!

Called many things—a humorist, an inspiration, a story-teller, a motivator and a few others that can't be mentioned here—Billy delivers simple principles for success that he has proven over and over in his own life.

He is convinced that they will work in your life, in your business, and at any time . . . making the journey to the top not only simple but a whole lot of fun too!

He can be reached at:
Jubilee Enterprises International, Inc.
Post Office Box 506
Broken Arrow, Oklahoma 74013

918-455-3595   918-451-9536 fax
www.BillyRobbins.com   billy@billyrobbins.com

Jim Stovall

Jim Stovall has been a national champion Olympic weightlifter, a successful investment broker and entrepreneur. He is Co-Founder and President of the Narrative Television Network, which makes movies and television accessible for our nation's 13 million blind and visually-impaired people and their families.

Jim Stovall hosts the Network's talk show, "NTN Showcase," with high-profile guests. The Narrative Television Network has received an Emmy Award and an International Film and Video Award among its many industry honors.

NTN has grown to include over 1,200 cable systems and broadcast stations, reaching over 35 million homes in the United States, and NTN is shown in eleven foreign countries. NTN programming is also presented via the Internet at NarrativeTV.com, serving millions of people around the world.

Jim Stovall joined the ranks of Walt Disney, Orson Welles, and four United States presidents when he was selected as one of the "Ten Outstanding Young Americans" by the U.S. Junior Chamber of Commerce. He has appeared on "Good Morning America" and CNN, and has been featured in Reader's Digest, TV Guide and Time magazine.

He is the author of *You Don't Have To Be Blind To See*, as well as *Success Secrets of Super Achievers*, *The Way I See The World*, and his new book *The Ultimate Gift*. The President's Committee on Equal Opportunity selected Jim Stovall as the 1997 Entrepreneur of the Year, and he was honored to be chosen as the

2000 International Humanitarian of the Year, joining Jimmy Carter, Nancy Reagan, and Mother Teresa as recipients of this honor.

He may be reached at 5840 South Memorial Drive, Suite 312, Tulsa, OK 74145-9082, or by e-mail at JimStovall@aol.com.

Possibilities I

Awakening Your Leadership Potential

Get your copy of the first Oklahoma Speakers Association anthology released in 1999 from the author you received *Possibilities II* from or order direct from:

>
> Oklahoma Speakers Association
> P.O. Box 701918
> Tulsa, OK 74170-1918
>
> *Possibilities I*
> ISBN 0-964120-8-4 $12.95 US per copy
>
> Fax order to 918-495-3626
> Email Jeff@JeffreyMagee.com

Name:_____

Address:_____

City/State/Zip:_____

Number of copies ordered:_____